GREATER BOSTON

METROPOLITAN PORTRAITS

Metropolitan Portraits explores the contemporary metropolis in its

diverse blend of past and present. Each volume describes a North

American urban region in terms of historic experience, spatial con-

figuration, culture, and contemporary issues. Books in the series

are intended to promote discussion and understanding of metro-

politan North America at the start of the twenty-first century.

JUDITH A. MARTIN, SERIES EDITOR

GREATER

BOSTON

Adapting Regional Traditions to the Present

illustrations by the author

S A M   B A S S   W A R N E R ,   J R .

University of Pennsylvania Press | Philadelphia

10 9 8 7 6 5 4 3 2 1

Published by
University of Pennsylvania Press
Philadelphia, Pennsylvania 19104-4011

Library of Congress Cataloging-in-Publication Data

Warner, Sam Bass, 1928–
    Greater Boston : adapting regional traditions to the present / Sam Bass Warner, Jr.
        p. cm. — (Metropolitan portraits)
    Includes bibliographical references (p.) and index.
    ISNB 0-8122-3607-6 (acid-free paper) —
    ISBN 0-8122-1769-1 (pbk. : acid-free paper)
    1. Boston Region (Mass.)—Civilization.   2. Regionalism—Massachusetts—Boston
Region.   3. Boston Region (Mass.)—Social conditions.   4. Boston Region (Mass.)—
Economic conditions.   5. Human geography—Massachusetts—Boston Region.
I. Title.   II. Series.
F73.7 .W37   2001
974.4'61—dc21

                                                                    00-066965

For Margaret DePopolo

CONTENTS

FOREWORD

Judith Martin

The Metropolitan Portraits series seeks to understand and describe contemporary metro regions in a fresh manner—one that is informed and informative. This task is being undertaken by a set of longtime teachers and observers of the North American metropolitan scene. Sam Bass Warner's *Greater Boston* begins this series more creatively than I might have imagined. As will be the case with future volumes, Warner here stresses the power of local cultures to give shape to metropolitan politics, to community life, and to varied ways of living. Like other contemporary metropolitan regions, Boston today faces daunting issues. Warner delivers a specifically Bostonian perspective on broadly shared metropolitan challenges, and also offers unusual insight into the character of this particular region.

None involved in this series knew precisely how to address our common challenge. Warner here creates a work of imagination, grounded in varied realities of daily life. Some of Warner's insights will ring familiar to local readers: labeling the Boston region "a city within a forest"; using Ipswich, Lawrence, Framingham, Natick, and the Cape Cod towns to illustrate current growth challenges; treating the ongoing importance of town life in the region as an underlying frame for understanding greater Boston. But much will surprise: Warner's claim that Boston's role as a national training center for all kinds of music creates an unusual undercurrent for regional cultural life; his description of the new openness in the region's economic life, based in part on changes in university admissions; his perspective that the large size of the region's public schools forces children to master a social setting that is more anonymous than most of their parents' institutions.

This book is not the "traditional" view of Boston. The region's newcomers—Brazilians, Cape Verdeans, and others—overshadow the familiar tension of Brahmin and Irish. There is little of politics-as-usual, rather a focus on the power of localism as a force for good and bad. Ordinary economic analysis is absent; instead, Warner describes the magnetism created by the agglomeration of venture capital, higher education, government-sponsored research, and a plenitude of innovating companies.

As a car-less Cambridge resident, Warner faced a special challenge in interpreting a region spread out 40–50 miles in diameter, with over 1.1 million more people than in 1950. His solution was to rely on more than one hundred local informants ranging widely over the Boston region, to add to his own long local knowledge and experience. This particular volume adds a unique visual component—Warner's own pen-and-ink drawings, which seek to convey both the ordinary and special characteristics of the Boston region.

To my mind, and I hope to readers', the power of a seasoned academic mind, and the creative force of art displayed here, combine to offer a new and exciting view of a region that has held a place in the American imagination for three centuries.

Introduction: Finding Boston

How do Bostonians live these days now that they have spread themselves over 4,200 square miles of eastern Massachusetts and southern New Hampshire? It is not an easy question to answer.

First, there are so many of us. The 1990 Census estimated 4.7 million, and ten years later we are probably 5 million. Then, of course, we are not all the same. We are young and old, men and women, prosperous and struggling, white, black, and brown, newcomers and long-settled residents. By commonplace labels the Boston mix departs a little from the U.S. average. We are a little more Caribbean, Puerto Rican, and Central American than Mexican, more Irish and French Canadian, Azorean, and Cape Verdean than elsewhere, and we have long been short on Germans and African Americans. We are, and always have been, a settling place for new immigrants. Taken altogether, the region is very mixed and is the nation's fourth most populous metropolis.

Confronted by such numbers and such variety, one person can hope to master but a few questions. In the work that follows five questions have guided me.

1. Is the distinctive New England institution of the town and the open town meeting still alive, and is it continuing to serve as a framework for many forms of local community life?

2. Who are the Yankees today? Who are the men and women who identify locally and who invent new institutions and modernize old ones, thereby keeping city and town traditions alive?

3. What is the nature of the new regional economy?

4. What might be a widely shared and distinctive example of popular culture in the Boston region?

5. How are Bostonians managing their dependence on their natural surroundings?

I sought the answers to these questions by reading newspapers, especially the regional editions of the *Globe*, and by talking to my fellow Bostonians. After such discussions I read the histories and background material my informants' concerns suggested to me.

Would it have been easier to describe the Boston region fifty years ago, before we exploded over the land and before we became so numerous? I think not.

During the 1950s the directions and possibilities of the post–World War II world were just revealing themselves. Most Bostonians in those days carried the memories and fears of the long local depression that had set in with the price collapse of 1921 and persisted, except for wartimes, until 1960. During those four decades most experienced a narrowing of the horizons of opportunity, and they responded with defensiveness. The popular wisdom called for sticking with your family, staying within your neighborhood and congregation, marrying your own kind, and grabbing for a secure base. The ever-repeated phrase was, "It's not who you are, or what you can do, but who you know that counts." So guided, most of us lived within small social cells whose margins proved tough and resilient. It was not easy, back then, for an investigator to move from cell to cell.

The authors of the times recorded the situation. No fresh winds of choice blew through Edwin O'Connor's settled Dorchester parish,[1] or Jack Kerouac's mill town,[2] or Robert Lowell's Beacon Hill and his grandfather's estate.[3] When the journalist John Gunther traveled through Massachusetts for his state-by-state political reports he found more fear of strangers and more narrow prejudice here than in most of America.[4]

Thomas O'Connor of Boston College, the leading historian of the city of Boston, thinks that World War II and the ensuing Korean War began the dissolution of the region's parochialism. Fascism discredited race and ethnic prejudice. War joined strangers together in common tasks, and the Korean War began the desegregation of the U.S. military and the effective civil rights movement.

The changes since my childhood and youth have been quite remarkable. As I ventured out beyond my small circle of acquaintances for this research, the strangers I talked with proved to be a wonderfully open and accepting group. In their separate ways they were fashioning a new Boston, a much more tolerant society than the ones that had preceded it.

Liberal we are now, but perfect we are not. Like everywhere else in the United States we have suburbs that zone and price themselves to exclude others.[5] New construction and new regulations, no matter how worthy, often face the response of "not in my back yard." We still have young people who band together in cliques and gangs to cover their uncertainty by put-downs and fighting over turf. Snobs and invidious comparisons abound because we are humans. We even have a few politicians who get elected by urging us to exclude. But for all these commonplace bad attitudes and antidemocratic behaviors, things are much better here than they were. Bostonians can live much more freely than before, even while carrying their favorite ethnic memories, and newcomers can expect a civil, if not always a friendly welcome.

The reader deserves two warnings about what follows. The research for the book, and its interviews, tables, and readings, were done during the years 1994–99. Of course, everything about the region is in motion: people's lives move on, companies have their good years and bad, public issues change. Thus, the details given here will not have remained fixed. My expectation, however, is that the core questions addressed here are of sufficient centrality to endure despite the lapping waves of change.

Finally, the illustrations demand some explanation. The drawings in this book are not, in most cases, pictures of items mentioned in the text. Instead they might best be thought of as a separate visual essay that sets before the reader an additional offering of regional details. The drawings are the work of an amateur draftsman. I include them because they have a quality that photographs lack: they require that the delineator spend three and four hours examining a particular scene. My hope is that by employing such an old-fashioned medium readers will be encouraged to linger at places where the Boston scene catches their eye.

Geography: What You See, What Was, and What There Is

The fall, late September and early October, is the best time to visit Boston. The hurricane season has gone by, the cold damp is not yet upon us, the days are warm and sunny, the nights are cool, the air is crisp, and the mosquitoes sluggish. There is often a bright southwest wind for sailing, the cities and towns are brimming with the young people who come each year to our schools and colleges, and the leaves on the trees are spectacular.

The scarlet and orange of the maples, the yellows of the hickories, cherries, and aspen, the papery brown of the beech, and the ocher, deep reds, and purples of the oak border every road and highway. These warm colors are often intensified by a contrasting green background of scattered clumps of pines and hemlock. Of course the busiest streets, the shopping malls, and the borders of apartments and stores are dreary stretches of asphalt parking whose dark grays are hardly relieved by the litter of advertising signs and electric poles. But most Boston streets, even city streets, are tree lined, and beyond the suburban malls are miles and miles of forest houses. Boston is truly a gathering of cities and towns in a forest.

The bright colors return each year because ours is a cut-over hardwood forest of stump sprouts and young trees. Ever since the Europeans settled here in the early seventeenth century the land has been cleared, cut, and recut. First the best trees were harvested for building ships and houses, then the rest was burned to make farm fields, and what remained was harvested for lumber and firewood, over and over again. The fast-growing character of cherries, aspen, birch, and maples makes them predominate at first, then, given time, the oaks come in, some growing to be our great trees.[1]

This deciduous forest gives another lovely moment in late April, but it lasts only a week or two, and its precise timing varies with our unsettled weather. It is a wonderful time when the flowering of the trees and their beginning leaves present a delicate screen of dots of yellow and red mixed among the pale greens of the starting leaves. The airiness of these small things makes the woods a breathtaking beginning to the warm season.

Does it seem strange that an American city—one of the oldest and densest settled places in the United States—might be a forest? Look down from an airplane: trees, ponds, and the ocean are all that you will see when the leaves are out. Drive the highways and look about. Even in the old cities and dense suburbs inside the circumferential highway (Interstate 95, also Massachusetts Route 128), the planted streets and yards make a canopy to shelter us during all the months from spring to fall.

Your highway atlas gives another picture, and it is not incorrect. It shows today's Boston to be a region of 204 cities and towns in Massachusetts and southern New Hampshire joined together by a half spider web of highways. The 1990 population of this city region was 4,667,000. At the northern and western edges of the region, Interstate 495 forms a half circle that runs from the Atlantic shore to central Massachusetts, from Newburyport on the north to Hudson on the west. The region then follows the Rhode Island boundary south to Rhode Island Sound, and east to Cape Cod and Massachusetts Bay. The inner circle highway, I-95 and Route 128, makes the inner band of the spider web. It runs shore to shore, from Gloucester on the north to Braintree on the south. Across these highway bands run spokes radiating out from their hub at the city of Boston. These new

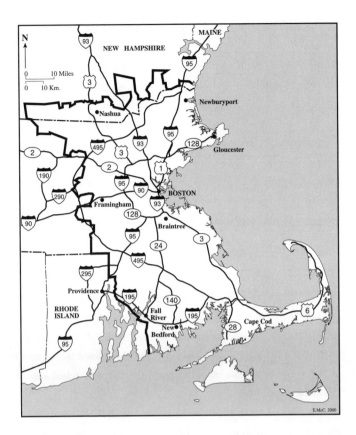

Map 1. Greater Boston

superhighways, all constructions of the years since World War II, are repositioning our homes and businesses, spreading things out, making distant connections commonplace. They have knit together 4,200 square miles of cities and towns that formerly were organized in a sort of planetary hierarchy of city, suburbs, mill towns, and rural villages. Now the domination of the old city of Boston and the largest mill towns is weakening, and clusters and subcenters of all kinds are springing up along the highway spider web. It is a new pattern, very much the pattern that now dominates all North American cities.

This region composes a Boston that never existed before. It is a social and economic unity whose boundaries have been established by the daily commuting patterns of its residents. These comings and goings establish a city region that takes in all of Cape Cod and the Islands, all of eastern Massachusetts to the edge of Worcester County, and extends north to the southernmost tier of New Hampshire cities and towns. There are, of course, alternative definitions of the region. The *Boston Globe* with its Sunday supplements covers a slightly smaller eastern Massachusetts territory of 3.8 million. The U.S. Bureau of the Census adds Worcester to form a Boston Consolidated Statistical Area of 5.5 million. And a case can be made for adding all of Rhode Island and most of New Hampshire to make the metropolitan unit embrace a settlement area of 7 million. It seems likely that adding Worcester, Providence, and the heart of New Hampshire to Boston would tax the imagination and defy the experience of many Bostonians who are already having difficulty forming a full regional outlook. Instead, common sense directs us to accept the 4.7-million-sized settlement, a definition that rests on the everyday actualities of two giant circumferential highways: Interstates 495 and 95.[2]

It is difficult for a driver in the eastern United States to know whether the highway in front of the windshield might be in New Jersey, Pennsylvania, or Massachusetts because the layout of these giant new roads conceals the human settlements. These highways were built to save money, not to inform motorists. Because the roads demanded such quantities of land, swaths a football field wide, the engineers tried to save property and earth-moving costs by putting their new roads where no one was, in old woodlots and on abandoned farms. Look to your right and chances are you will see the road skirting the slope of a forested hill, only a bit of the hill's edge scraped away to make the road itself. To the left something that looks like a clearing in the forest most often proves to be the shrubs and grasses of a swamp. The new interstate highways are a lowland tour of eastern Massachusetts with an occasional cut through a narrow valley between two hills. For the same reasons of economy, the highway stays away from the ocean side. So, no matter where you drive, ring or spokes, it is all forested hills and wetlands. Only occasionally a warehouse or the edge of a city pokes through, but the forest is everywhere.

Unlike the West, with its distant mesas and mountains, this is not a landscape anyone can master at sixty miles per hour. The land is a patchwork of small events, a quick change in the slope of the hill, a sudden appearance of a brook, the spread of a great tree. It is a walking landscape, and very available now that in most places the forest is sufficiently advanced so that it chokes out the brambles and shrubby underbrush. For those on foot there are remnants of old farm roads, lines of low stone walls, the surprise of old apple trees, even daylilies and vinca from abandoned house sites, occasional outcroppings of ledge that bring sunny openings to the forest cover, and every kind of wetlands from ponds to shrubby marshes. This sort of land and its forest await any child's imagination. At the forest's edge shrubs screen the interior, which, once penetrated, often holds a scattering of rocks and boulders, bits of moss and ferns, fallen branches and trees, and especially in spring, brooks everywhere that call forth dams and sluiceways.[3]

The land that is today's Boston city region is the ongoing product of slow and ancient processes. It is the outcome of the very making and remaking of the earth's crust, and it is the product of the faster change of the advance and retreat of glaciers. There is something curiously fitting in the land's geological histories. Here is a region of people who once set themselves off as unique, and who as Bostonians still pride themselves in some specialness. What could be more appropriate than to now learn that the rock upon which all this pride rests was once neither Europe nor North America? Both Pilgrim Plymouth and Puritan Boston rest upon the ancient stones of what we today call the Avalon Belt, or Zone.[4]

Six hundred million and more years before the present, the land underlying a major segment of the Boston city region came into being. The area, some of whose remnants are still visible, lies to the east of a line running approximately from Ipswich on the northeast to Narragansett Bay on the southwest. Gloucester, Salem, Lynn, Boston, Quincy, Brockton, Taunton, New Bedford, and Plymouth all rest upon this old construction. At the time of its building it was not connected to North America. Rather, it was part of a chain of mountains and islands much like the islands of Japan or the Aleutians. The land welled up in volcanoes and hot magma from a subterranean zone where the ocean floor was sinking beneath the arc of new islands. The chain, the Avalon Belt, or Zone, stretched from Newfoundland to North Carolina and was separated from North America by ocean. Some of the granites we all encounter give evidence of this ancient land-building process that went on for several hundred million years.

Now much of the Boston city region rests on this ancient sloping platform of volcanic rocks and granites whose ages fall between 625 and 590 million years prior to our time.[5] This basement of rock is so very old that it has lost its picture-book volcanic appearance due to subsequent erosions, invasions, and continental collisions. For instance, ancient Precambrian weathering formed the sedimentary rocks we call Roxbury Pudding stone, rocks easily identified as the building stones of many of our late nineteenth-century Richardsonian churches. The Blue Hills, too, are a revelation of a long aging process. Because granite is formed by slow cooling beneath the surface of the ground, the Quincy granites of the Blue Hills must have been buried under a deep burden of material that slowly weathered away to expose the underlying granite hills we now use as a southern landmark of the city of Boston.

The Avalon Zone itself subsided in time, a process we can recognize in the form of the basin of harbor and land that makes up Boston and its adjacent suburbs. The same process created the Nar-

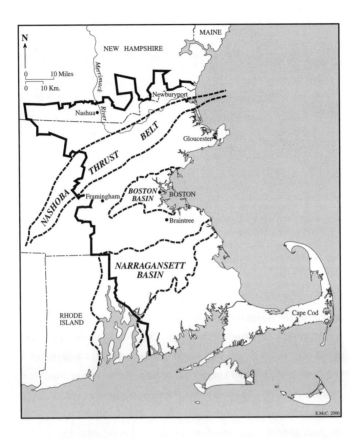

Map 2. Geology of the Region

ragansett Basin, which stretches south and west from Brockton to
Fall River, Taunton, Providence, and Narragansett Bay. The whole
rock Avalon basement tilts to the east so that much of it lies buried
under hundreds of feet of sand and gravel. The immense accumula-
tions of sand and gravel are themselves the product of millions of
years of erosion and glacial rearrangement. In Cape Cod the burden
varies from two hundred to six hundred feet,[6] and seaward it under-
girds the miles of Atlantic shelf whose best-known local feature is
the Grand Banks fishing grounds.

Turn of the Merrimack at Pawtucket Falls, Lowell

These later events are crucial to an understanding of the land that makes up the Boston region. As the ancient chain of islands pressed against the North American continent, the pressure formed a belt of tilted hard stone ledges that begin in Massachusetts at Webster in a narrow belt and then spread out to be miles across at Worcester and Marlborough. Then as the belt curves north and east to Lowell and Newburyport it narrows once again. This band of rocks, called by geologists the Nashoba Thrust Belt, has been invaded by melted granites. A remarkable subsequent consequence of the belt appears in the turning of the region's largest river, the Merrimack. The Merrimack flows due south from its origin in the mountains of New Hampshire until it meets the Nashoba Thrust Belt at Lowell. There it turns abruptly east to follow the margin of the belt to the Atlantic Ocean.[7] Then, years after the forming of the Nashoba Thrust Belt, about 300 million years ago, the collision of the North American and African continents crushed the Avalon Zone into the American continent, where it has remained steadfastly attached ever since.

Much of the visible landscape of Greater Boston is the work of comparatively recent times, the past two-and-a-half-million years.

Glaciers blanketed the northern half of the continent during these times, advancing and retreating perhaps as often as five times. The immense quantity of water frozen into glaciers lowered the level of the sea by about four hundred feet, while the burdensome weight of the glaciers deformed the earth's northern surfaces so that they lay about three hundred feet below their current elevation. Like some giant waking from a sleep, the postglacial uplifting and stretching of the formerly depressed land brought a succession of earthquakes.

Eastern Massachusetts continues to be one of the most active earthquake zones in the northeastern United States. Research dating back to sixteenth-century observations has established a steady rate of small and medium tremors. The biggest one in the recorded series came on November 18, 1755, when Professor John Winthrop of Harvard College reported that many "chimnies were leveled with the roofs of houses, and many shattered and thrown down."[8] Geologists now puzzle over the possibility of another such serious event. Several hypotheses have been put forward to explain these intraplate continental tremors, but none so far fit the site and timing records well enough to allow any prediction. As a precaution against a still possible major quake, builders of large structures are required to install earthquake bracing. Prediction or no, the many small quakes continue. Recently, one centered near the active Newburyport area (2.7 on the Richter Scale) awakened North Shore residents in early January 1999.[9]

The glacier's grinding of the surface rocks and its dragging of soil, sand, stones, and boulders along its pathways rounded off the preexisting hills and filled valleys. These movements also made new hills and land forms. About 16,000 years ago the earth warmed once again and the glaciers began to melt, retreating backward toward the north as their leading edges melted. The resorts of Cape Cod and the islands of Martha's Vineyard and Nantucket are glacial dumps, terminal moraines, piles of material that geologists call till, which the glaciers left behind. Southeastern Massachusetts, the flat areas of ponds and bogs, is an outwash area, a place where streams of meltwater spread clays, sand, and gravel out into a wide plain. The thickness of these glacial layers varies enormously—in some places it is several hundred feet deep, in others only a few feet, and in some places the rock has been swept clean and remains exposed.[10]

Glaciers also built hills. Often till, sticky with clay, would mound up and a subsequent glacial advance would ride over the heap, rounding it off and shaping it in the direction of the glacier's advance. The Boston region is littered with such hills, drumlins. The islands in Boston Harbor and many hills in the city are of the same origin: Bunker Hill, in Charlestown, and the hills of the siege of Boston, Dorchester Heights in South Boston and Fort Hill in Roxbury. These were the sites where the Revolutionaries placed their cannon in March 1776 to force the British to evacuate the city. Maps show seventy-four drumlins within the suburban ring that runs from Newton and Lexington eastward to Lynn and Hull and Boston Harbor.[11]

Beneath the glaciers ran rivers of meltwater whose channels swept up sand and gravel into long drifts. These eskers, so called, are often mined today for their sand and gravel. Locally, the most famous of these was the Needham esker, located on what is now the Needham Industrial Park next to I-95. For thirty years its contents were carried off on a railroad to make the land that is now Boston's fashionable Back Bay section. Often, too, large chunks of ice would become buried under the glacial till and outwash so that the sunken block only melted after the surrounding debris had settled and warmed. The result was a pronounced depression where the old ice block once sat. These kettle holes can be found everywhere in the woods, and some were even large enough to form ponds. Round Pond in South Truro is such a kettle, as is Kingsbury Pond in Norfolk.[12]

The final historical process in the making of today's Boston city region records the interactions of European and later immigrants with the land itself. The scouring of old hills of stone left the region with a poor, acidic soil[13] that is often so mixed with small stones that the gardener who picks the rocks off the surface soon discovers that down below there is some malevolent force that sends up an ever-fresh crop. In some places, large rocks and small boulders are so numerous and so strewn together that farming and even grazing is impossible.

It was this poor soil and the railroad that together drove agriculture from the Boston region. The railroad brought inexpensive food and produce in from the West, while the poor soil made the local farms uncompetitive. Today only cranberries flourish, while some orchards, vineyards, and vegetable gardens survive in scattered farm sites: apples in the Nashoba Valley to the west, the cranberry bogs and truck farms and vineyards in the southeast, and to the northeast in Hamilton, Beverly, Ipswich, and Topsfield gentleman farms and horse farms still present a pastoral landscape.

Farm abandonment and forest advance commenced many years ago. The 1840s were the agricultural peak of the region. At that time three-quarters of the land stood either as pasture and under cultivation or as town and city buildings, streets, and roads. Forty years later commentators began to notice the forest's advance, and by 1920 the forest had regained perhaps half the territory. Today open fields and farms make up about 5 percent of the region's surface, the urban forest covers 65 percent, and the remaining 30 percent is lawns, pavement, and roofs.[14]

The old rock and newer glacial configurations of the present Boston city region can be usefully understood as having five distinct land form areas: the sunken Boston Basin, the northeastern up-

Temple Road, New Ipswich, N.H.

lands, the central spine of hills, the southeastern lakes district, and the long Atlantic shoreline.

The first area, the sunken Boston Basin, is composed of the city of Boston, its harbor, and an adjacent bowl of towns. Its surrounding uplands even today offer startling views. A motorist leaving Boston, heading south on Blue Hill Avenue, arrives at the crest of the road at Franklin Park, where the panorama of the Great Blue Hill appears in the distance. If, however, you leave the city on the Massachusetts Turnpike (I-90), the ascent of the road is gradual, but high retaining walls and steep roadside banks announce to you that the land is rising with the hills and uplands of Newton. To the northwest Route 2 has been cut through the rock escarpment at the top of Belmont Hill so that the sharp rise of the highway nicely defines the rim of the basin. Similarly I-93 headed north cuts through the rock of Stone Hill in Medford to give a similar view. When drivers approach the city on either path, the road offers dramatic views of miles of rooftops and a distant palisade of office towers that now rest upon the sites of the early Puritan settlement.

The uplands beyond the Boston Basin are not uniform. The second area, a northeast quadrant—the area north and east of Route 2 from Concord and Ayer to the boundary of New Hampshire on the north, and to Salem, Gloucester, and Newburyport on the east—consists of rolling country of modest hills and extensive wetland. The land fluctuates between fifty and a hundred feet above sea level.

The third area is a higher and rougher spine that extends westward across the region, roughly paralleling the Massachusetts Turnpike (I-90) on its north edge; on its south an approximate boundary line might be drawn from Sharon to Milford. Here are steep hills and drumlins interspersed with wetland valleys. The range of altitude varies between one hundred and two hundred feet.

The fourth area lies to the south and east of this spine. The lands fall off into what might be called Boston's "lakes district," the low-

Cranberry Bogs, Lakeville

lying and slightly undulating glacial outwash plain of ponds and bogs that characterizes southeastern Massachusetts and Cape Cod.

The fifth area, the Atlantic shore, is very much the handiwork of the glaciers. Here the human settlements have been as contradictory as any urban process. The melting glaciers left the outwash beaches of southern Massachusetts from Westport to Wareham, the terminal moraines of Cape Cod, the Elizabeth Islands, Martha's Vineyard, and Nantucket. The sandy beaches on the South Shore from Sandwich to Marshfield, and on the North Shore from Essex to Salisbury, are similar: eroded sands and glacial outwash that the ocean has formed into sand bars, barrier beaches, narrow lines of open beach, and small hills of glacial till. Two segments, however, are different. The South Shore from Scituate to Weymouth and the North Shore from Nahant to Rockport are characterized by granite outcroppings, boulders, and ledges that strike out at right angles to the shore, allowing only crescent beaches to form between the rocks.

This long southern and eastern shoreline edge of the Boston region alters the local weather by dividing the region into two climate zones, shore and inland. In general Boston weather comes from the west, giving it a continental climate of hot summers and cold winters, six months of warm, six months of cold. The ocean, however, adds special effects to this general pattern. The cold ocean water in the spring makes for a delayed warming in April and May along the coast. Summer winds blow up from the southwest, bringing the heat from the southern states. In the fall, occasionally, the hurricanes of the Caribbean, instead of following an offshore track, turn inland to flood the shoreline, level the forests, and tear up the electric power lines. Hurricanes are not frequent, but they can be very damaging, as they were in 1938, 1954, and 1955. In the winter the counterclockwise swirl of all Northern Hemisphere storms can draw in the cold, wet air from the North Atlantic in severe gales of rain and snow, what are called northeasters here from their wind direction.

Yet the ocean also brings many delights. Along the South Shore of Buzzards Bay and Cape Cod the shallow water and nearby Gulf Stream warm the water to 70 degrees for swimmers. On the north side of Cape Cod and all around Massachusetts Bay, however, the water is cold, even in the shallows, so that swimming is for the hardy. But this cold water, part of a large circulating swirl from Nova Scotia, brings summer relief in the form of afternoon onshore breezes. The city of Boston's famous "East Wind" off the harbor is but a downtown version of the breezes that blow all along the coast. The ocean also brings the soft summer fogs when the warm air from the southwest flows over the cool air that lies on top of the ocean water. As the temperature of the warm air falls, myriad droplets of moisture form, and a fog suddenly engulfs everything in its cool embrace.[15]

Like the forest that conceals an agricultural past, the resort and retirement shoreline communities cover over a history of shipbuilding, commerce, and fishing. Many of these towns throve during the eighteenth and nineteenth centuries as builders of wooden ships, and many carried on an extensive coastwise and distant commerce: Taunton, Boston, Medford, Essex, and Haverhill were once shipbuilders as well as traders. Fall River ran overnight boats to New York

City until the New York, New Haven and Hartford Railroad built its present shoreline route in the early twentieth century. New Bedford flourished as a whaling port from the close of the Revolution until the discovery of petroleum in Pennsylvania in 1857 from which kerosene for lamps could be made. Salem rivaled Boston as a port for trading to the West and East Indies in the eighteenth and early nineteenth centuries. Steam engines, steel ships, and railroads foreclosed this commerce, but some remnants survive. Old merchant warehouses, narrow portside streets, and charming old houses now stand as outdoor museums to attract thousands of tourists to the old ports.

The fishing industry has been the last of the old economy to fail. Every shoreline community from Fall River around Cape Cod and Massachusetts Bay to Newburyport engaged in ocean fishing, seining inshore, dragging for nearby bottom fish, and seeking the cod of Georges Bank. Seagoing factory fishing and packing plants from Europe, and later intensive modern electronic fishing by New Bedford and Gloucester fleets, have finally fished out the vast schools of nearby fish. Today the U.S. government and representatives of the fishermen debate the setting of quotas in the hope that decimated species might restore themselves. Restoration is a complex problem because it involves much more than leaving a few species to multiply; rather, restoration requires helping to get the whole ocean ecosystem back into a fertile balance. The plight of these local fishermen stands as a warning to the still-thriving Pacific Northwest and Alaska fisheries. Fish of all kinds are still available in small quantities, the lobsters are still not wiped out, and the scallop and clam beds are not all polluted, so the local cuisine can still boast of the pleasures of wild creatures from the sea and shore. Yet still another disaster of exploitation looms: the extensive lobster population is likely to collapse due to overfishing.

The destruction of the offshore fish is a fitting metaphor for the overconsumption of the shoreline itself. Here the first Puritan settlers left a misguided legacy with their law concerning the owner-

Toward Beachside Houses, Scituate

ship of shorelines. Their legislation, which has persisted, held that the owners of shore property owned the land down to the line of mean high tide. That is, private landowners effectively controlled the edge of the sea itself. This conception is quite unlike the rules of Roman law countries like France and Spain, or Spain's colony, California, where the beach is public. As a result of this unfortunate Massachusetts law, private owners of seaside property have been able to exclude their urban neighbors from using this important natural resource. Like the overfishing of Georges Bank, the walls of summer houses that line beaches and the prohibitions of seaside owners have prevented the region from developing these wonderful gifts of nature.

In the late nineteenth century, however, perhaps owing to the Boston region's intensive urbanization, a preservation movement sprang up to counteract the private acquisition of the natural and scenic resources of the state. The Society for the Preservation of New England Antiquities and the Trustees of the Reservations were established in 1891 as companion eleemosynary institutions to receive and even to purchase historic and scenic properties.[16] At the same time, supporters of these private initiatives established the public Metropolitan Park Commission (1892) to set out parks and parkways and to recapture and restore the beaches of Boston and surrounding towns. As a result, the walls of privatization have been breached in significant ways. The Metropolitan District Commission (successor to the Park Commission) owns and manages miles of shoreline and edges of the Charles, Mystic, and Neponset rivers. The Trustees operate very popular public beaches on the North Shore and Martha's Vineyard, and the Commonwealth of Massachusetts also maintains important public beaches in Salisbury, Plymouth, and Martha's Vineyard, while the federal government owns and manages a long stretch of the south side of Cape Cod.

Elsewhere, however, private ownership reigns. The houses and yards of the shoreline owners range from large, tasteful spreads that fit into the landscape to the more common lineup of houses against the beach. Moreover, in this climate of artificially created scarcity, the shore towns have declared their public beaches to be reserved for the exclusive use of local residents. It is not sufficient to be a citizen of the United States or the Commonwealth of Massachusetts, although both entities protect and even on occasion maintain these shores; you must be a town resident.

THE REGION'S URBAN GEOGRAPHY

The geologic forces that shaped the forest and the shores of the Boston region also established the pattern of its initial settlement. Today's Boston city region is but the latest expression of human uses for the inherited land. In 1990 there were twenty-one cities and towns in the region whose population was 50,000 or greater. All save the suburb of Malden are located at the sea or along an important river. All save Brockton and Nashua, New Hampshire, were settled before 1660. The early settlements owe their beginnings to the fact that in the seventeenth century water was the only easy mode of transportation. Also, seaside and river towns offered marshes and wild grasses for cattle. Thus, the glacial forms of shore, river course, and uplands established the initial European settlers' pattern, which in later years of urbanization grew and shifted with the changing economy and new patterns of living.

City building is always a process of bit-by-bit additions so that the lineaments of the past continue to assert themselves directly and indirectly. Many railroads followed the river's edge, and then the highways paralleled the railroads. The airport lies at the edge of the city, but the city is still the passenger's destination. Because of this recurring process of mixing present and past, it is convenient to mark the geographic history of the Boston region with three period labels. The first era is that of the domination of the sea and the rivers, the years from 1600 to 1870. The second era is the time of the domi-

Map 3. Towns with 1990 Population Greater Than 50,000 and Settled Between 1622 and 1700

nation of the railroad and the newly paved streets, roads, and state and U.S. highways of 1870–1960. The third era is the time of the limited-access freeways and the new interstate highway network, 1960 to the present.

The first era, 1600 to 1870, is marked by the power of the land and the slowly advancing urban system, which grew out of the largest settlement, the port of Boston. Boston Harbor is the largest and best in the region and was the initial destination of the great wave of English settlers, the 20,000 who came in the first decade after 1630.

The harbor's shores and rivers quickly filled with farms and villages. On the north, the towns of Medford and Chelsea bordered the Mystic River, which drained some of the northeastern uplands. The Charles River, whose meandering route carried it through the central spine of hills, found settlers in Cambridge, Watertown, and Waltham. On the southern edge of the basin the Neponset River, which drained some of the southeastern lowlands, supported the villages of Dorchester and Milton.

Elsewhere fishing and trading ports along the coast attracted settlers who planted the beginnings of the region's cities: Newburyport, Salem, Lynn, Quincy, New Bedford, Fall River, and Taunton. All these towns engaged in shipbuilding, and all traded along the coast of North America and to the West Indies. During the eighteenth century the string of North Shore ports from Salem to Newburyport even rivaled Boston in their extensive ocean commerce.

The Revolution, however, brought significant changes. Taunton, mining the bog iron nearby, cast cannon for the army and began its progress toward becoming an important center of metalworking.

Turner Street, Salem

The Quakers of Nantucket, harassed by American Revolutionaries and the British alike, settled among their mainland compatriots from Providence, Rhode Island, to New Bedford. With the coming of peace they started New Bedford on its path to becoming the whale oil capital of the world. Meanwhile, when the Tories fled Boston, with the British army's evacuation of the port in March 1776, merchant families from Salem moved to Boston, thereby strengthening its dominance. What followed from the Revolution, then, was two urban systems in the region, which are just now being unified into one Boston-based system.

In the southeast, Taunton flourished during the nineteenth century as a center for the manufacture of locomotive and railroad equipment, the casting of stoves, and the making of silver plate and alloy tablewares. Fall River established fast overnight boats to New York City. New Bedford flourished as a whaling port until the discovery of petroleum in Pennsylvania in 1857 ended its control of lighting oil. All these towns were part of the Providence and New York trading system. Indeed, both Fall River and New Bedford became important cotton textile towns, extensions of Providence's Blackstone Valley concentration. Later, after the textile collapse of the 1920s they became home to many New York–oriented garment shops.

Elsewhere Boston soon established its dominance. In 1793 Boston merchants who wished to get control of trade with the farmers and new settlers of New Hampshire built the Middlesex Canal. It passed through the Mystic River and its lakes to a junction with the Concord River, which then carried the canal to its meeting with the Merrimack at present-day Lowell.[17]

The same motive led to a brief speculation in turnpike companies. During the first decades of the nineteenth century, these companies built toll roads that bounded over hills and across valleys in straight lines toward their destinations, regardless of the topography. To the north, the Newburyport Turnpike began across the Mystic River on Broadway at the harborside town of Chelsea and then ran

Stone Mills, Fall River

northeasterly to Topsfield and Newburyport. To the south, Washington Street, Boston, was extended to Dedham, Walpole, Attleboro, and Providence. To the west, Boylston Street, in the suburb of Brookline, was the origin of a turnpike to Framingham and Worcester.[18]

The rivers flowing into Boston had been used from the very first to power gristmills, sawmills, and rag paper mills; to full wool and process tobacco. In 1813, a consortium of Boston merchants built on the Charles River at Waltham the nation's first integrated cotton mill. Theirs proved a successful copying of contemporary English machinery. The Charles River, however, is a modest stream that suffers from occasional summer droughts when the flow virtually ceases. After their successful Waltham prototype, the investors looked for a more powerful stream. The nearby Merrimack offered the possibility for the large-scale exploitation they were seeking. The Merrimack has twenty times the flow of the Charles and is a river whose flow can be managed to sustain a summer volume. Its origin lies in central New Hampshire at Lake Winnipesaukee. The Boston Associates thus could supplement low summer flows by drawing down water from the lake.[19]

In 1822 the work began for a new built-for-purpose town at the junction of the Middlesex Canal and the Merrimack. Investors raised a dam and laid out canals parallel to the river to carry the water power to factories that in time would line the canals: first Lowell and then a string of mill towns, Lawrence, Methuen, and Haverhill in Massachusetts and Nashua and Manchester in New Hampshire. In time Manchester became the site of the world's largest cotton mill. All along the Merrimack and its tributaries there gathered a hive of textile mills and related industries for dyeing, finishing, printing, and making textile machinery. Boston capital controlled the lot.

The Boston-based economy also expanded with the shoe and leather business. Shoemaking in Massachusetts had often been a winter job for farmers who picked up the makings in the city, worked the leather into shoes, and then returned the finished products to Hawley Street dealers in downtown Boston. The town of Lynn, where English tanners and skilled shoemakers had settled in the seventeenth century, had become, by the time of the Revolution, a significant cluster of small handworkers' shops. A succession of inventions for sewing leather and joining tops to soles (the Blake sewing machine in 1858, the McKay stitcher in 1862, the Goodyear welt machine in 1864–67) turned this old handicraft into a midcentury factory process. As mechanization advanced, shoe factory sites radiated outward from the Lynn center to Boston itself; Haverhill on the Merrimack; Marlborough to the west, on the Assabet, a tributary of the Merrimack; and to the southern city of Brockton, on a branch of the Taunton River.

These early specialties of textiles and shoes and their related industries at first scattered across the region wherever a river or stream offered the possibility of a dam. This early industrialization process was facilitated by the employment of mechanics to build and repair machinery in all the mill towns. Soon an army of skilled men furnished the improvements and inventions that led to still more machines for making all manner of commonplace items from

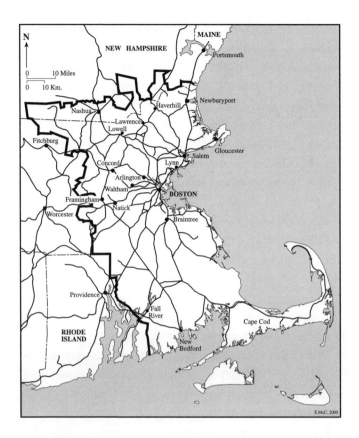

Map 4. Regional Railroads, 1882

shovels to hats. In this first phase of industrialization, the Yankee tinkerers and the Boston capitalists often prospered together.

The second period, from 1870 to 1960, was one in which the urban system freed itself from such strong dependence on seaports and rivers. The coming of the railroad and the coal-fired steam engine both knit together the many small mills of the region and also changed factory work from small mills to big factories. Mills employing tens and hundreds grew to factories employing hundreds and thousands. The small city of many factories and the small town beneath the big factory became characteristic of the second era. The wall of six- and eight-story brick mills along the Merrimack in Lowell and Lawrence and the giant United Shoe Machinery factories in the small towns of Beverly and Whitman, the Draper Loom Company plant in Hopedale Village, and the American Woolen plant in Marlborough dwarfed the houses and tenements of their workers. Boston and its suburbs of Cambridge, Somerville, Waltham, Everett, and Chelsea, thanks to steam power and the railroad terminals nearby, grew to be one interrelated industrial center. Someone built a textile mill in East Boston near where Donald McKay had built his clipper ships, and a huge shoe factory settled down in suburban Roxbury. Foundries, oil refineries, glass, soap, and candy factories, slaughterhouses, and piano factories joined the old portside sugar refineries, lumberyards, wool, cotton, and leather warehouses, and fish-processing plants. This was the era when the Boston Basin functioned as the industrial metropolis of the region, the factory planet around which satellite mill cities moved.

It is difficult today to recapture a sense of the intense reticulation of the late nineteenth- and early twentieth-century railroad network, which sped passengers, freight, and mail back and forth between formerly scattered river towns. In part the railroads re-etched the existing pathways. The Boston and Providence went straight to Providence like the turnpike before it. The Boston and Albany followed the Worcester Turnpike to Natick, Framingham, and Worcester. If you wanted to go to New York City in 1880 you took the Old Colony Railroad to Fall River, and then the night boat. The Newburyport Turnpike had not been a town builder, so no railroad duplicated its path. Instead, the Eastern Railroad and the Boston and Maine joined the North Shore towns from Lynn to Gloucester and then branched north to the Merrimack towns.

Such were the main pathways, the railway lines that earned the city its sobriquet, "the Hub." These were the routes now duplicated by the radial highways leading out of Boston. But within the region of Greater Boston you could, with a little patience, travel by railroad from one place to almost any other because railroads, large and small, crisscrossed the mill town region. You could go from Concord to Boston by way of the Arlington suburb on the Middlesex Central Railroad (now the Minuteman bicycle path), or to Waltham and then to Boston on the Fitchburg Railroad. From Framingham you could travel southeast to New Bedford on the New Bedford Railroad, or you could go next door to Marlborough on the Fitchburg line. You need not go through Boston to get from Lawrence to Salem; the Eastern Railroad would carry you there directly.[20]

A long secular depression set in with the price collapse of 1921 and lasted in the Boston region until 1960 and the flowering of the new high-technology and service economy. Textile mills and shoe factories began their southern and overseas migration in the 1920s until these industries became a small fraction of local manufacturing. As the mills left, chronic unemployment settled upon the mill towns. Lynn, Salem, Lowell, Lawrence, Marlborough, Waltham, New Bedford, and Fall River suffered intensely, and in time what had been a high-wage region became a place of lower than average wages. In the 1950s you could hire a physicist or a secretary or a machinist at lower wages in the Boston region than the prevailing rates across the nation.[21] The empty mill buildings, however, did furnish cheap space for new start-up companies. Once again the Charles River proved an unanticipated pathway.

The Massachusetts Institute of Technology, founded in 1861, opened its doors on the edge of the fashionable new section of Boston, in Copley Square in the Back Bay. In half a century it had grown so that it required much more space. In 1916 it moved across the Charles to its present location on Massachusetts Avenue, in Cambridge. Here the university sat on the edge of Cambridge's concentration of varied industries. As a school of technology and a land-grant college, MIT took as its mission to study science and to harness science to technological applications for contemporary

Map 5. The Boston Region—North

industry. At the time of its move its specialties were chemistry, metallurgy, electric power, and civil and mechanical engineering. Half a century later the core of MIT had shifted to physics, mathematics, aeronautical engineering, and all branches of electronics. Over these fifty years the professors and graduates of MIT became the new inventing class in the region, replacing the machinists and tinkerers of former times. King Gillette, the inventor of the safety razor, typified the old ways; Vannevar Bush and Lawrence Marshall, radio tube and radar men, symbolized the new.

During World War II a tremendous demand for electronics nurtured the MIT companies, forcing them to find new quarters. They followed the handiest route, the path of abandoned and underutilized mills along the Charles River. After the war, still newer companies spread out from Waltham and Needham along a new highway that the state had built to relieve the crosstown automobile traffic that was then clogging the main streets of what were then the outer suburbs. This road, enlarged several times in the 1950s and 1960s, became the highway symbol (Route 128) of the new economy and the new decentralized ways of the Boston city region.

What is new about the geography of the third period, the time since 1960, is its spread-out and scattered quality. Warehouses, fac-

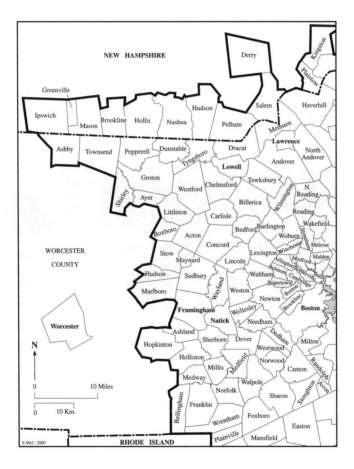

Map 6. The Boston Region—West

Map 7. The Boston Region — South

tories, office buildings, stores, and malls sprinkle themselves along the rings and spokes of the highway spider web and take up open land wherever a road offers a convenient connection. Employees have responded by commuting in every which way across the network. The work that now leads the regional economy is now very different from its predecessors. General Electric makes jet aircraft engines in Lynn; the city of Boston hardly knows manufacturing,

CHAPTER 1

but Harvard University, MIT, and the major hospitals are larger employers than the former giant, the United Shoe Machinery Corporation. Digital Corporation surpassed American Woolen, one of whose plants it occupied in Marlborough. By the same token, the highway and road network, its maintenance, and the cost of the cars and trucks that clog it far exceed the investments in the former railroad system.

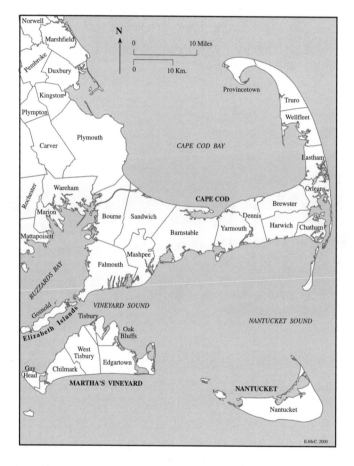

Map 8. The Boston Region—Cape Cod and the Islands

The years since 1960 have seen an extraordinary transformation, and what happened here has been happening across all of North America. The special local event has been the effects of the outer interstate highways. Their extension through southeastern Massachusetts has finally joined that area and its cities of Taunton, Fall River, and New Bedford to the Boston orbit. These same highways have also promoted an extraordinary boom on the shores of Buzzards Bay and in Cape Cod and the Islands as resort and retirement areas. The meanings of these new arrangements are by no means clear, even now. What they foretell for urban life, and what the continuing interpenetration of older patterns will bring about, together form the subject of this book.

How We Make Our Living

It is difficult to characterize so varied a hive of activity as the gathering of businesses and institutions that compose the city region of Boston. Some businesses are as intimate as the work of the young mother who cares for another's child, or as individual as the handyman who looks after a few apartments. Other businesses hire thousands of clerks who labor on computers and telephones for banks and mutual funds. Some of us tend franchises to replace tires and mufflers, others of us go to hospitals where there are a myriad of jobs as different as nursing patients and struggling with insurance bills; and although there are no automobile plants here anymore, there are large factories where men and women tend machines and assemble everything from catheters to rockets.

One way to capture such diversity is to imagine the region's businesses as characters assembled for a group picture. In your mind place them side by side in a cheerful photograph, much as the Chamber of Commerce might. Economists make such pictures all the time. They want to sort out the short from the tall, the scrawny from the sleek, the scruffy from the well-tailored. Such a snapshot of the Boston region would resemble Table 1, a listing of what Bostonians do.

For the past century the region has been growing more and more to resemble the national averages in employment and industries. Like the rest of the United States, we have ceased to be a region of

	Boston Region*	United States
Total Employment	2,176,000	124,900,000
		percentages
Agriculture, forestry, fishing	0.40	3.0
Mining	0.04	1.0
Construction	3.00	6.0
Manufacturing	15.00	16.0
Transport, communications, utilities	5.00	7.0
Wholesale and retail trade	25.50	21.0
Finance, real estate, insurance	9.00	6.0
Services	42.00	35.0
Business	—	6.0
Personal	—	3.0
Entertainment, recreation	—	2.0
Professional	—	24.0
Public administration	—	5.0
Unclassified	0.06	—

SOURCES: For the region, U.S. Bureau of Labor Statistics, unpublished data; for the U.S., *Statistical Abstract of the United States: 1997* (Washington, D.C.: Government Printing Office, 1997), table 648.

*Excludes the first tier of cities and towns in New Hampshire. The regional analysis does not include the self-employed or public service employees.

farmers and fishermen and a workshop of factories and mill towns. We are less and less concentrated in manufacturing, more and more attending to the personal services of education and healthcare and more and more busy with finance and business services. We are fast becoming that amorphous gathering of salespeople and staff that economists call the service economy. Yet, such categorizations, like the group portrait where everyone stands still for a moment, hide what really goes on here.

An opening key to an understanding of the Boston economy is the realization that the region possesses few resources save water and people. Yes we have abundant rain, there is nice scenery and an adjacent ocean and lots of stone and gravel to build with, but these are hardly the resources that generate wealth these days. Our resource is people, the people who live here and the people who move here. To build on such a resource our businesses and their workers must step lively, and they must welcome new people and new ideas. To be sure, there is much continuity with the past; old firms and old industries persist, but to live so long they must find ever new paths.

Consider banking. It is at once the stodgiest and the most daring of businesses. Boston can boast of venerable banks and spectacular bankruptcies. Even now, amidst our successes, local banks are prey to national conglomerates. Yet the State Street Bank has found ways to prosper from the times of clipper ship merchants to the present moment of global computer trading. Some years ago the bank took up the business of processing securities and of keeping records for money managers, mutual funds, and pensions. It built a suburban office building in the adjacent city of Quincy to handle the new lines. This mundane accounting in turn complemented its own banking and fund management so that this staid provincial bank has become one of the region's big employers with 7,300 workers. Its success makes it very much a contributor to the money-management tide that has flowed in recent years toward Boston, thereby making it a leading financial center.[1]

The new technology, of course, is everywhere, but sometimes it takes unanticipated forms. John F. Keane, a Harvard graduate, sold IBM mainframe computers to corporate clients. As he went about and talked with his customers, he noticed that few companies had been able to link their computer capabilities with their business goals. In 1965 he gathered a dozen employees and began consulting with a very special approach. Keane and his staff work with their corporate clients to set goals for the integration of the client's computer systems with the client's business plans. The Keane company only gets paid as the new systems meet these agreed-upon goals. Such down-to-earth ways, the ability to keep promises in a timely fashion, have proved a bonanza to the firm. Although there are larger and wealthier information technology consulting firms, Keane has proved a national winner.

For example, the firm was chosen to manage a technical help desk when Microsoft introduced its Windows 95 operating system, and it did the same later for Hewlett-Packard's printers and plotters. Recently it established information systems so that Toyota Motor Sales and the 3M Corporation could keep track of their thousands of parts and varied products. It set up patient management information banks for Massachusetts General Hospital and the Robert Wood Johnson University Hospital. Here the firm's skill in bridging the awkward time when both the old and new systems must be kept up and running proved essential. The company was pressed into service to alleviate the problems that arose when the zeroes turned up on old computers, quite by surprise, at the commencement of the year 2000. From its center city location, the firm now deploys 9,000 workers at forty branch offices throughout the United States and Canada. Altogether, the thirty-odd years of continued success has left John Keane saying, "I'm surprised, myself." [2]

EMC Corporation, on the I-495 ring at Hopkinton, typifies the uncertainties of computer manufacture. Richard J. Eagan, who continues as chairman, and Roger Marino started the firm in 1979 to supply add-on memory boards for microcomputers built by Digital, Wang, and Data General. Disaster stuck in the late 1980s when a shipment of faulty drives from Japan almost drove the company out of business. The faulty materials compelled the firm to spend a year and a half repairing their clients' broken-down computers.

After the crisis, the company switched products to make disk storage machines for IBM mainframes. They perfected a storage system, which consists of dozens of disk drives that are linked one to another so that the nest of drives holds an enormous quantity of data. Moreover, the disks are so arranged that the most frequently consulted material rests in temporary storage. Thereby the machine can quickly retrieve this information without searching through all the files. The storage system now lies behind the operations of airline ticketing, auto rental reservations, automatic teller machines, and bank records. EMC proved so successful with these machines that IBM was challenged to manufacture its own unit and to start a price war.

A lithe firm, as survivors must be, EMC then shifted its efforts toward developing storage networks that would allow all the computers in a company to make use of central storage, whether the computers be desktops, minicomputers, or mainframes. Such networks required the provision of a great deal of software, a whole new enterprise for EMC. Indeed, the company's sales efforts these days tell customers that the software and the storage units are more important to an effective business than any particular brand of computer. As a result of this latest adaptation EMC now enjoys a measure of safety from outright manufacturing competition.[3]

Keane and EMC are examples of Boston's high-technology life, but the region's economy is in no way narrowly specialized. Some of our most successful businesses are adaptations of very old lines to which bits of Yankee ingenuity have been applied. Malden Mills, justly famous for its responsible labor policies, thrives in the old New England line of textiles. Staples, Inc., of Westborough has established a chain of large office supply stores that have changed the scale of the stationery business through computer inventory control.

T.J. Maxx, a Framingham discount clothing business, seems just to have used care and executive skill to prosper. In this case, Ben Cammarata, an experienced New York garment district manager, was hired in 1975 by a Boston discount store chain, Zayre Corporation, to establish a clothing chain. After choosing a base in Framingham, Cammarata took a no-frills approach. His stores would rent only inexpensive space near the malls, but they would not struggle with the high rents of prime locations. The clothes themselves were to be well-advertised brand names—clothes advertised by someone else. They were not to be in-house manufactures, nor would the stores try to cover a full range, like a department store. Cammarata's skill in selection and low prices are the T.J. Maxx formula for success. While others in the discount trade stumbled in the early 1990s downturn, the firm prospered. In 1995 it purchased a major competitor, the Andover-based Marshalls. By November 1997 the enlarged T.J. Maxx had $6.7 billion in sales from 1,200 stores.[4]

The surprises are seemingly endless. A sleepy eighty-year-old Medfield maker of public clocks, Electric Time Company, is suddenly awash with orders. Mall designers and Main Street rejuvenators have decided that pillar clocks, the kind that used to decorate our streets, and public clocks set on the gable ends of buildings, make an attractive focus for retail spaces. Or, a local express company, AEI, has taken a point from the taxi business. It operates its Boston services with small delivery trucks that are owned by their drivers. Or, because of the *Exxon Valdez* tanker catastrophe, petroleum shippers are now seeking giant tankers with double hulls. The long-closed Quincy shipyard is attempting to reopen to build such vessels.[5] In Wilmington a small company, Solectria, part laboratory, part factory, turns out a hundred electric cars and trucks each year and supplies appropriate machinery to other companies while the big automobile makers fuss and dither over having to make electric cars.[6] Meanwhile, Converse Rubber and Stride-Rite Shoe companies, long-standing manufacturers, ride the tossing seas of fashions that alternately favor and spurn their makes.

The snapshot of the Boston regional economy, thus, must capture both the new and the old as they pass by in the parade of change. An independent corporation established by the Commonwealth of Massachusetts to assist the state's economic development provides an annual account, which it calls *Index of the Massa-*

Shipyard Workers' Homes (1919), Arnold Street, Quincy

chusetts Innovation Economy. It nicely captures the blending of the new and the old. It points out that Massachusetts is one of a cluster of high-technology states. Its sisters are California, Florida, Illinois, Minnesota, New Jersey, New York, and Texas. Of these it is the "most research and development intensive economy in the country and is more highly reliant on federal funding to support this activity" than any of the others.[7] During the cold war, military contracts fueled the Boston region's economy, but now such work has declined. For 1997, the specialties of the Boston region were financial services (119,000 employees), postsecondary education (78,000), innovation services, engineering, testing, and so on (78,000), computers and communications hardware (77,000), software and communications services (77,000), machinery, materials, and industrial support (58,000), textiles and apparel (41,000), defense (36,000), and healthcare technology (31,000). In all of these groupings Massachusetts is more concentrated than the nation, and it has twice the national average commitment in postsecondary education, computers and communications hardware, textiles and apparel, and defense.[8]

Such a summary of specialties gives a fair sense of the uniqueness of the Boston economy. It cannot, however, reveal what makes it take this form. To gain a sense of how the region now prospers it is essential to recognize the strong brew of human ingenuity, sustained work, and unexpected moments of good fortune that bring new businesses into being, and which continued success requires. Many stories of this kind await an investigator of the Boston region, so I have been forced to make a selection. I have chosen a few firms whose specialties represent both the new economy of high technology, finance, and services and the old traditional concentration on textiles and shoes.

Boston Scientific is not the sole creation of John E. Abele, but its story can be told through his experiences. In 1997 the firm had become a large, publicly traded company of many divisions. That year it had 12,000 employees at plants in Natick, Watertown, Miami, Spencer (Indiana), Minneapolis, San Jose, Ireland, and Japan. Since then it has been busy purchasing its competitors, trying to match its size and weight to that of its conglomerating customers, the HMOs and medical fusions of America's healthcare industry. Of course as it grows ever larger, it begins to suffer all the problems of lack of supervision and control of its new purchases.[9]

John Abele, a founder, was born in New London, Connecticut. His father served as a submarine commander whose ship disappeared in 1942 off the Aleutian Islands. The widow moved the young family to Newton, where she taught violin in the public schools. In these childhood years, between the ages of five and eight, John suffered from osteomyelitis, a staph infection. He was operated on three times, and during his second stint at Children's Hospital his doctors tried the new wonder drug, penicillin. It didn't work, but was tried again for the third operation. One thousand two hundred shots later, Abele had somehow recovered. In his association with the leading physicians of the city he sensed something that would later be an essential insight for his life's work. He came to realize that "in a sense, all doctors are experimenting on their patients. They are trying to apply the lessons learned from others to their patients' specific problems. Thus, they are either trying something new or adapting something known to a fresh situation."[10]

When he was fourteen he went to work after school in an old-fashioned hardware store, a place of boxes, drawers, and bins holding a myriad of tools, parts, and fixtures. In time the owners allowed the boy to do more than tend the stock. In retrospect, he found his center in that store: he loved the treasure trove of parts, he loved talking with the customers, and he loved helping them to solve their problems.

In 1955, he graduated from Newton High School and went on to Amherst College to major in physics and philosophy. His grades and his interest fluctuated with his relationships with his teachers.

He had a bad physics teacher, so he rejected physics as a possible career. When he graduated in 1959 he was one of a special group of 5 percent of the seniors who had not signed up for some kind of graduate school. He decided to work before committing himself to a particular career. After many interviews he secured a job under the tutelage of an experienced district representative to sell lighting for an Ohio manufacturer. It was a great opportunity to see many possible occupations. From such a sampling he found his life's path, a brew of gadgets, inventions, and relationships with people.

One of his customers was a small medical instrument company, Advanced Instruments of Newton. This company made one fine instrument, an osmometer, that accurately measured the concentrations of fluids. Its major application came in the testing of kidney diseases. Abele transferred to Advanced Instruments after a year. He began reading up on physical chemistry, and he sought out a retired MIT chemistry professor who had invented an artificial kidney. In short, he began his career as a salesman-teacher to his customers, the very pattern that now shapes the Boston Scientific sales staff. By 1965 he had risen to be general manager of this small firm of thirty people. The owner, however, did not want to expand the business, so John moved on.

Now he wanted to purchase a company of his own. But to support his family, while he shopped about, in 1967 he joined the Technical Education Research Center in Cambridge as a consultant. TERC then had a contract to train people for new kinds of jobs. Abele took on the biomedical field. He discovered that the U.S. Air Force had some protocols for the technicians who maintained and repaired medical equipment. Abele helped to set up training programs to match the protocols. Today, there is a new civilian occupation, biomedical equipment technician (BMET), with approximately 8,000 members who gather each year for a professional convention.

He had a partner, a former Advanced Instruments colleague,

Patrick Alessi, who was a manufacturing man. Together they searched for a small firm to buy. They found what they were looking for in the basement of a closed rectory in Belmont. Here was the lair of an inventive genius, Itzak Bentov, a Czech Jew whose family had been murdered by the Nazis. Bentov had migrated to Israel, where he designed guns and rockets for the Israelis. A man of many interests, a plastics manufacturer in Leominster, Massachusetts, had brought him to America to work on polymers. In 1969 he had invented a steerable catheter tube that can be used to navigate an artery or give access to an organ. Such little tubes are at the heart of today's effort to design less invasive surgery. Bentov had a partner, a man associated with the business research firm of Arthur D. Little in Cambridge. They were seeking someone to manage and sell the catheter. Abele and Alessi agreed to take on the job on the condition that they might buy the new firm at a later date.

Operating by the name of Meditech, the pair set up a new business in 1970 in a small brick building at 372 Main Street, Watertown. Here they rented 900 square feet encumbered by the furnace. After a long search for capital among various sources in Boston and New York, through the good offices of a boutique investment banker, they chose an informed investor, a medical firm, Cooper Laboratories.

For the next ten years they carried on in the Watertown basement, expanding floor by floor until they had taken over the whole of the small building. The firm grew 20–25 percent each year, and the partners plowed all the profits back into expansion and into inventing new variations on their products. Alessi proved very effective at setting up new methods of manufacture and devising incentives to keep productivity up. Bentov's original catheter formed a kind of technological platform upon which the firm built a family of ever-changing products. This cluster of related devices was continually generating new applications and new accessories, and the steerable catheter continued to be sufficiently unique and innovative that it was hard for competitors to copy.

For his part, Abele continued his career as a salesman-teacher, visiting physicians, listening to their problems, getting a sense of the goals of their practice and their research. Physicians, like most professionals, focus their lives on an area of expertise, and limit their input of information to the range of their special concerns. In this professional setting Abele was like a worker bee, visiting everyone. His became the bridging role among physicians, and back and forth to his firm's designers and manufacturers. Today Boston Scientific trains its thousand salesperson-teachers to adopt this role and also to be careful to observe the rules of confidentiality so that they do not leak research secrets from one laboratory to another. By the 1970s the young firm had formulated its mission statement: "Develop technology, products and procedures that reduce risk and trauma, time and cost." Such a statement seems a truism in today's climate of medical cost-cutting and efficiency, but a quarter century ago when it was announced it upset many physicians because they feared it would compromise patient care. Cost, back then, was not a topic to be discussed.

In the years 1978–79 John Abele and Peter M. Nicholas formed their partnership. They were neighbors in Concord, had children the same age, and as they met on family errands they began to share their experiences, Abele's with Meditech, Nicholas's with Millipore in Bedford. In time they decided to team up, Abele continuing with sales and development, Nicholas with finance. They formed a new corporation, Boston Scientific, mortgaged their houses one more time, and bought out Cooper Laboratories' interest in the former company.

Continued growth had forced the firm into new quarters in Watertown, and by 1981 it had outgrown its Coolidge Hill Road location. The partners located an empty woolen mill, the old Phoenix Mills, on Pleasant Street, next to the Charles River. But in 1981 the possibilities of preservation had not yet captured bankers' imaginations. The partners couldn't find a bank to finance purchase and remodeling. Instead, Peter Nicholas worked with the Commonwealth of Massachusetts to help it set up an economic development bank, and through that program Boston Scientific was able to acquire 100,000 square feet of textile mill. The main building had been erected in 1919 on the site of the former Bemis cotton mills, sailmakers to the U.S.S. *Constitution*. It is a heavy timber and brick factory, a part of which dates from the eighteenth century. Now carefully cleaned and modernized, it is a dynamic mix of new and old. Although some of its workers use high-tech machinery, they assemble the medical products by hand in batches because the product designs change so rapidly that no mechanized production line would be appropriate.

Abele likens this plant to an early woolen mill, a place where people without much education can get a start. The ethnicity of the nearby residents is Italian, Armenian, and Asian, but at one point when the personnel department did a count, there were sixty nationalities on the company payroll. The firm offers many courses in English as a second language. The special feature of working here is not merely its open entrance but also its possibilities for advancement. Work is done in teams, and in all segments of the business there is a need for leaders and coaches. They are vital to the training and sustenance of the teams who must cope with an endless stream of ever-new materials and processes. In 1994 the company expanded further, relocating its headquarters to Natick, along State Route 9, where it took over a former brewery and transformed it into a modern office park.

Abele thinks a new culture is being formed out of the necessary mode of this business practice, a culture of continuing innovation and adaptation. The salesperson-teachers are the crucial makers of the new cultural ways because they carry the ideas back and forth between the parent company and its thousands of users.

Parametric Technology Corporation of Waltham exemplifies Abele's culture. It is an extremely innovative software company whose sales technicians, support personnel, and developers are in continual interaction with the engineers who are its clients. The company doesn't really make anything. Its costs of materials are but 2 percent of the product: software. The software line is a special family of computer-aided design tools (CAD), in this case particularly fine three-dimensional projections. Like Boston Scientific, the firm owes its origin to an immigrant, a Russian professor of mathematics, Samuel P. Geisberg.

Boston is, after all, the home of Ralph Waldo Emerson and his homily of the better mousetrap. The popular phrasing of this homily runs, "If a man can write a better book, preach a better sermon, or make a better mouse-trap, than his neighbor, though he builds his house in the woods, the world will make a beaten path to his door." This version, fittingly enough in these days of Boston versus Silicon Valley competition, seems to have been a California improvement of words Emerson delivered at a San Francisco, or Oakland, lecture of 1871.[11] What Emerson did not mention was the necessity for Bostonians to keep their society open so that they could attract talented foreigners and their new ideas for traps.

Geisberg came to the United States in the late 1970s and went to work for Computervision of Bedford, a firm Parametric purchased in 1998. Here he worked with pioneering CAD/CAM software. He left Computervision for a company called Applicon, where he proposed a three-dimensional application or package. The firm refused the project on the grounds that the turf had already been occupied by giant corporations like IBM, whose competition might prove fatal. At the time, however, the giants offered only two-dimensional software. Geisberg was told to develop his ideas on his own time.

He did. In 1985, Boston venture capitalists extended him $5 million in start-up funds. He formed a publicly traded company, Parametric, and successfully launched his three-dimensional system, which he called PRO/ENGINEER. It is used at engineers' work stations to make initial designs and to subject those designs to functional analysis. Further, the user can consider alterations through

CHAPTER 2

simulations that trace the effects of the proposed change upon all the other elements in the object. Next, the programs allow engineers to make accurate computer models whose dimensions are sufficiently tight to be used for setting up machining, making molds, and planning assembly. Of course, once in production, the product can continue to be experimented with on computers in order to judge the effects of future modifications.[12]

The company proved profitable from its very first year and has expanded rapidly ever since. Now it has settled in Waltham, next to the Brandeis University campus. The total workforce in 1997 was 5,051, of which a thousand men and women are at the Waltham headquarters, with the remainder scattered across the nation and the world in 254 offices and training centers. Research and development teams are based in Waltham, Minneapolis, San Jose, Salt Lake City, and Haifa, Israel, and Pune, India. Important as these designers are, the key to the business now lies in the hands of the applications engineers and sales representatives who visit and work at the customers' sites. There they study the customers' processes in order to furnish suitable software packages. The customers are whoever does mechanical designing: the automotive and aircraft industries, electronics manufacturers, furniture companies, medical equipment makers, and the like.

Parametric is venturing into a new field. It is developing networking systems that will enable members of a worldwide company to share specifications, manuals, and vital engineering data, regardless of their geographic location. Parametric consists of hardworking and highly skilled teams, but here once again they face the competition of giant information technology corporations in America and Germany.[13]

Hologic, another Waltham-based firm, is a classic local company, a star among the firmament of small companies started by MIT graduates. In this case the technical innovator was Jay Stein, a 1968 Ph.D. While a student, he worked with Bruno Rossi measuring x-ray emissions from stars, and after graduation he joined a firm Rossi and a colleague had established, American Science and Engineering. There, Stein explored various possibilities for commercial applications of x-ray measurement. One opportunity followed on the assassination of President Kennedy and the reappearance of terrorist bombs. The Post Office requested machines to inspect packages. Stein invented such a device, and it is still in use. It is not, however, the machine that inspects your baggage as you move toward your plane at the airport.

By 1980 he was anxious to go his own way. Like Abele, he wanted to have a company of his own. He teamed up with the American Science and Engineering vice president for sales and marketing, David Ellenbogen. Working in a small space on Bear Hill, Waltham, next to Route 128, they developed a system for intravenous geography. Squibb and Company swallowed the start-up whole, purchasing the company in 1982 on the condition that the founding pair stay on the job for at least three years. This practice of large firms absorbing small beginnings before they get a chance to be established is very common here in the Boston region. Indeed, the region has become a kind of start-up meadow for the feeding of large national and international corporations. Some worry that this rapid consumption prevents beginning firms from developing here and thereby adding significantly to local employment.[14]

In 1986, however, the team of Stein and Ellenbogen made a fresh start. Having arranged for an infusion of venture capital, they began their new company, Hologic, to manufacture and market x-ray machines that could accurately measure bone density. The firm soon became extremely successful, and now employs 350. Their main focus is upon the widespread disease of osteoporosis, the progressive loss of bone. The loss advances with age, and the disease particularly attacks women. Today it is estimated that there are twenty-five million cases in the United States alone, but only 5 percent are diagnosed and given satisfactory treatment.

In the first years the company's sales went mostly to Europe, where the disease was being treated with hormones. The Hologic machine offered physicians an effective way both to diagnose and to follow the progress of the treatment. In 1994 the U.S. government authorized Medicare reimbursement for such x-ray diagnoses, and in 1995 Merck and Company received approval for a new drug, Fosamax. Since then Hologic's sales have boomed in the United States as well as Europe.[15]

As is common in all high-tech firms, the initial product served as a platform for the development of a family of related products. The first machine had been designed to be placed in a physician's office, but the further elaborations offer a range of options. There are ultrasound bone analyzers, and a small model that gives approximate readings from testing a patient's heel density. The firm has also acquired a company in Illinois that makes fluoroscopes to help surgeons with noninvasive operations on the small bones of the neck, hands, and feet. Stein and Ellenbogen have also spun off a small company that makes a device to detect bombs in luggage, even plastic ones. Sales, here again, are mostly to Europe since the United States has yet to adopt such strict procedures for its baggage. Today Hologic is one of two companies in the United States that manufactures bone density measuring devices, and it seems well situated to expand its range of tools for physicians.[16]

Jay Stein entertains a different view of some aspects of Boston's culture than many who lump all high-technology undertakings into one group. His is not a computer software experience, nor is it inextricably tied to little shifts in clinical practice as is Boston Scientific. Instead he bridges two of the large specialized groups here in Boston. He belongs to the group of physicists and engineers. His work, however, leads him to work with physicians to develop machinery that they can use easily and efficiently. In these two cultural settings Stein experiences the engineering world as one of reason and argument. As he puts it, "In engineering the boss tries to convince the underling about the correct way to do things. There is an exchange of ideas. The mutual expectation is that the truth will come out."

In medicine the clinical tradition prevails. It is a tradition that sees medicine as an art, and therefore the experience of the skilled physician carries special authority, something above and beyond the data that two observers might agree upon as the facts. In a region like Boston with its many hospitals, clinics, and medical schools this professional division means that there are alternative traditions at work and in conflict here, even in the many shared fields where science and engineering intersect with the goals of clinical practice.

Stein also shares with many commentators a comparison between Boston and the Silicon Valley. He spends a lot of time in California because his suppliers and competitor are there. "The trouble with Boston," Stein says, "is that it has all the things necessary for innovation, but California has much more. California is much more entrepreneurial. Risk-taking is a positive experience there. The Boston establishment has a fear of risks. Boston investment groups are judgmental, not Californian. The question there is, 'Can you make us money?' " Just the same, he is a great admirer of MIT because he says it fosters excellence. "It has an equalitarian outlook. It doesn't matter what your race or religion." [17]

The necessity for social openness pertains as forcefully to financial institutions as to universities like MIT. The admission of Jews to full participation in Boston's banking, investment, and corporate law firms only followed the discrediting of anti-Semitism in the wake of Nazi persecution. Throughout the twentieth century, as opposed to most of the nineteenth, Jews in Boston were systematically discriminated against: refused land and homes in some neighborhoods and towns, their children set upon in schools, forbidden election to many clubs and associations, held to strict quotas at Harvard College, and restricted to a narrow compass in medicine, law, and banking.[18] During World War II Boston even suffered an anti-Semitic riot. The breaking of these barriers has been an important event in the reenergizing of Boston as a national financial center. A notable example of the postwar liberation of the city has been the successful modernization of Putnam Investments, one of the city's largest fund management houses.

The Putnam firm traces its name back to Judge Samuel Putnam (1768–1853), a longtime judge on the Massachusetts Supreme Court (1814–42). In Samuel Putnam's day, ship captains employed trustees to manage their property while they were at sea, and, as in our own time, the management of estates for widows and children was also an issue of great importance. In an 1830 case, Harvard College and the Massachusetts General Hospital attacked the management of a large estate of which they were the ultimate beneficiaries. The trustees had continued the donor's practice of large investments in the stock of early textile companies, and the stock had fallen in value. Harvard and Mass General wanted the trustees to make up the losses. Judge Putnam refused their appeal and in so doing enunciated the important "prudent man rule" for all fiduciaries.

The judge wrote: "All that can be required of a trustee to invest, is, that he shall conduct himself faithfully and exercise a sound discretion. He is to observe how men of prudence manage their own affairs, not in regard to speculation, but in regard to the permanent disposition of their funds, considering the probable income, as well as the probable safety of the capital to be invested." [19] In ensuing years Boston became famous, even notorious, for its trustees' careful management of family trusts. Indeed, during the long regional depression that set in after World War I, many economic commentators shared Jay Stein's assessment that Boston's money managers were too fearful of risk to provide the necessary capital for new business ventures.

A century after the judge's rule, his great-great-grandson, George Putnam, founded the present company in 1937 to offer mutual funds in common and preferred stocks to small investors. The company prospered with the post–World War II economy, its funds posting gains with the bull market of the late sixties when the Dow Jones index headed for its first 1,000-point reading. At that moment, in 1969, Putnam Investments hired Lawrence J. Lasser, a young Harvard Business School graduate who would in time become its modernizing chief. Lasser is a Jew, born in 1942, just a year before Boston's wartime anti-Semitic riot.[20] Raised in the New York suburb of Scarsdale, he later graduated from Antioch College in Yellow Springs, Ohio, and went on to the Harvard Business School, where he prepared for a career in advertising. He imagined such a job would give him a chance "to express his creative Antioch self."[21] For a time the military draft for the seemingly endless Vietnam War led him to continue his educational deferment as an instructor and case researcher after he had received his MBA in 1967.

While in business school, he and a group of his fellow young instructors fell to discussing stocks, making picks, even forming temporary investment pools. Their successes with the rising market suggested an alternative career goal. It seemed to young Lasser a delightful prospect to imagine being paid to make stock choices for others while also investing one's own funds. New York City, too, had lost its appeal. In 1968 and 1969 the city was in deep molt. Riots, street crime, and financial collapse seemed to threaten even prosperous Manhattan. Lasser imagined that if he took a Wall Street job he would be forced by the high rents to share an apartment on First Avenue with three others. Boston now looked more attractive. He sent his resume around to all the local mutual fund houses. At the time they seemed like small Yankee places to him, but he hit it off with the head of the research department at Putnam when he interviewed there. The day he was hired, Lasser said, "was the proudest day in my grandfather's life."[22]

The year Lasser joined Putnam as a securities analyst the firm was operating eight mutual funds, seven of which held equities only. The total value of the funds stood at $1.6 billion; the Dow Jones Index stood at 800 at the end of that year. Soon after he started, changes began to transform the firm. In 1970 the Putnam family sold its holdings, the vast majority of the shares, to a large insurance brokerage firm in New York, Marsh and McLennan. One of the hopes of the purchasers was that Putnam's new venture into the management of pension funds would continue the growth of the firm even if the stock market refused to rise. The pension business did, indeed, prove a fortunate addition, because during the stock market doldrums of the 1970s the pension payments continued to roll in so that by 1982 Putnam's mutual funds had risen only to $2.5 billion, while the pension funds stood at $7.5 billion.

Meanwhile, Boston's leading firm, Fidelity, introduced a number of changes that later would prove popular with mutual fund investors. Fidelity's sales were so lackluster in the 1970s that it began selling shares of its funds directly from its own offices instead of only through brokers. It also added money market funds as well as offering customer check writing. Fidelity, like all the mutual fund houses of the era, continued to manage its funds by the star system, assigning one publicly identified leader to watch over each mutual fund. The young Lasser slowly discovered the flaws in this then-universal system.

After five years Lasser was promoted to assistant manager of the Securities Research Department, and in 1975 to manager. From this vantage point he began to question current practice. The mutual fund business then concentrated almost exclusively on stocks. "Bonds are for sissies," fund managers were fond of repeating. Under the star system and its isolated cells of individual funds, if someone within a fund made a good pick of a stock, even if it were appropriate to other funds, the suggestion was likely to die at its place of origin. Moreover, despite the efforts of the groups within each fund cell, the star received all the credit when things went well, and all the blame when they didn't.

The Putnam firm carried this structure over to its pension fund business. Here managers took care of a bundle of ten accounts. So, as the business grew star managers were needed for each decennial increment. When to hire? When six new accounts had come in? Eight? Wait until the full ten? And there were more difficulties. Inevitably some pension fund managers did better than others. The corporate customers then began to make invidious comparisons and to demand each performance match the best one.

Additional difficulties revealed themselves in time. Far at the bottom of the firm hierarchy stood the salesmen, wholesalers as they are called in the trade. They were little regarded because it was thought that the key to the business was a good investment performance. If the fund managers shone, then Emerson's maxim could be relied upon to attract customers.

Fortunately for Putnam, during the mediocre 1970s Lawrence Lasser used his position in securities research to master, more and more, the business methods of an investment house. Then, suddenly, in 1980–81 one-fifth of Putnam's executives were hired off to other firms or left to set up their own businesses. Some left because compensation schedules had been kept too low; others took a few pension accounts with them to set up financial "boutiques," small firms with a salesman and a few accounts. The recovery of the Dow Index suggested a comfortable future for boutique managers. On December 31, 1982, it closed at 1,047.

All these departures brought middle management to the top to cope with low morale and the confusion attending the executive exodus. At first, a kind of two-man governance prevailed. Lasser took charge of the then-thirteen mutual funds and their marketing and sales. Another man tended the pension funds. The pensions, however, continued to suffer from their management contradictions. In 1985 Lasser was appointed chief executive officer, and he immediately reorganized the company.

As he recalls the 1982–85 years, he remembers asking what his business school training suggested. The starting question was, "What sort of business is Putnam engaged in?" The first answer was a negative one. "We are surely not in the investment performance business." A good record for the funds was only part of the answer. Slowly he came to the formulation that Putnam was a service business for institutions and individuals who were saving for retirement. Americans were living longer, and increasingly mutual funds had become an effective way for them to save. Examined in this service light, the burden on the company was to respond to the variety of the customers' saving strategies and to give good service throughout the life of the connection.

The reorganization upgraded the sales force. Salesmen became full partners in the enterprise. In return, Lasser expected continuous feedback from them about what customers were seeking. At the same time, to call attention to an energized firm, he multiplied the number and kinds of funds Putnam offered. There would be all kinds of income funds, capital growth funds, mixed income and growth funds, tax-free funds, bond funds, money market funds, overseas funds, and so forth. At present Putnam offers 110 different ones.

The multiplication of funds could only have been achieved by closing down the star system. There is, and was, no way to locate 110 investment stars. Instead, the goals and methods of each fund were carefully described and its decision rules set down. In this way investors could match their preferences to a particular fund, and Putnam's investment teams could put the right picks in the right places. Instead of the old fund-by-fund cells, research and investment teams gathered by specialty: some followed small firms, others big corporations; some specialized in particular industries, others tracked bonds; some have a domestic focus, others an overseas one.

Finally, to serve the growing numbers of individual and institutional clients, the question-answering and record-keeping branches had to be much enlarged. Currently there are 5,000 Putnam employees in its offices in Franklin, Quincy, and Andover who give customer service. The investment and sales force numbers another fifteen hundred.

The service concept and the team reorganization have been very successful. Putnam is now regarded as a very reliable and high-quality performer. Its funds have floated happily upward as the Dow rose from 1,000 to 9,000, while the volume of business expanded from $10 billion in 1982 to $278 billion in 1998.[23]

In 1998, Boston investment houses managed about $2 trillion of the nation's $3 trillion placed in mutual and pension funds. It seems as if old Judge Putnam had set a standard of honesty and reliability that, by some slow and unpredictable process, eventually earned Boston the trust of investors everywhere. And by a process clearer still, it is apparent that the energy and talent of newcomers like Lawrence Lasser have made the city and its funds American and world leaders.

Retirement savings is but one of the services that has attracted Boston innovators. Other entrepreneurs have fitted existing technology to an urgent social need and have succeeded brilliantly. The LoJack Corporation of Dedham is such an example. It sponsors a four-way symbiosis among new car owners, the police, insurance companies, and itself.

In the late 1970s and early 1980s Boston led the nation with its incidence of auto thefts, and the state as a whole supported a thriving population of thieves. Insurance rates rose to underwrite the heavy losses, while the police were derided by the citizens for their slow and uncertain recoveries. New car owners stood in special jeopardy. In 1978 William Reagan, a financier and former police commissioner in suburban Medfield, founded a company to combat theft through rapid detection. He imagined a radio transmitter in an automobile that might be activated and used by the police in the event a car had been stolen. He hired an engineer, Sheldon Aspell, who perfected a blackboard-eraser-sized transponder that could be hidden inside a car and activated through the police radio network. A

CHAPTER 2

The New Georgetown

transponder is a radio that lies dormant until it receives a designated signal. Upon receiving such a signal it begins to transmit a signal of its own. In the LoJack application, police cars are outfitted with tracking devices so that the officer in the police car can be informed of the distance and direction of the transmitting vehicle. Such a system could only work if the four parties bound themselves together. The LoJack Corporation energized the system by selling and installing the transponders to buyers of new cars. LoJack employees hide the transponder inside the car, and no notice of any kind is posted on the car. Thus, a potential thief has no way of knowing if the car is "wired." The identification of the transponder and the car is forwarded then to the central state police computer, which Lo-Jack supplies with continuing updates and appropriate software. Because of the rapid recovery and reduced damage suffered by stolen cars with LoJack signaling, insurance companies soon offered a 20–35 percent reduction in their rates to LoJack owners. Some insurance companies even donated tracking equipment to the police for the patrol cars.

Effective coverage came slowly. In 1984–85 the company demonstrated its methods to the Massachusetts state police. LoJack simulated eight hundred thefts, of which 95 percent were recovered within eleven minutes. The then-governor, Michael Dukakis, approved the system, and Massachusetts became the pioneering state for the tracking system. In 1986 the Federal Communications Commission allotted the company a police frequency, and LoJack commenced its diffusion. The company's strategy called for concentrating on big cities, wealthy states, places where new car sales and auto thefts congregate. Since the July 1986 Massachusetts beginning, the LoJack system has spread to car owners and police in South Florida, New Jersey, Los Angeles, Illinois, Georgia, Virginia, Michigan, New York, Washington, D.C., Texas, and Pennsylvania, and more are joining. Its success has also carried the system overseas to Europe, Latin America, and recently to licensees in China and Taiwan.

The expansion of the system requires some patience, since it rests upon adoptions by police departments, which are, themselves, conservative institutions. LoJack employs former policemen as its sales representatives, and it has tailored the use of its signals to good police practice. For instance, in order to protect an officer from a charge of false arrest, no search begins until the owner of the car files a formal complaint at a local police station identifying the car and alleging that it has been stolen. Also, a chase can be interrupted and resumed at a later time if a patrol car needs to attend to a more urgent matter. Such adjustments and expansion took time. Negotiations for adoption typically require two years, sometimes as many as eight. As a result the company consumed $30 million in capital before its first profitable year, 1989. The money for this investment came from "penny" stock issues on the Boston Stock Exchange, and from a large investment by the Union Carbide Corporation's pension fund.[24]

The LoJack innovation entails several unique processes. It does not endeavor to prevent theft by direct intervention. Yet, because professional thieves and chop shops have no way of knowing if the car they have stolen is a LoJack car, often the signal leads the police to the thief while he is in the car, or even to the chop shop garage or yard. The first step rests with the buyer of a new car, who must put up $600 for an installation. But as these buyers multiply, so do the hazards of thievery. As a consequence, the four-person symbiosis begun by the LoJack salesman and customer produces a widespread public benefit that spreads outward even to those not equipped. Car theft declines. In the Massachusetts case, the state has dropped from champion to the middle rank. Moreover, because of the lack of identification this program does not merely drive crime elsewhere, as many police endeavors do.[25]

Established electronic communication techniques and computers are the backbone technologies for both Putnam Investments and LoJack. Their innovations came from using techniques that were already well known. But innovation, technical or otherwise, is essential for success in the region. Two further examples show this process at work, even in the oldest of our industries, textiles and shoes.

The first example is Quaker Fabric Corporation of Fall River, a comparatively new firm that has found its niche within the old New England specialties of spinning and weaving. Quaker is one of a small group of very successful specialty firms that flourish in the region, companies like Malden Mills of Lawrence, which knits slivers (a ropelike material from the spinning process) in new ways to make the popular Polartec fleece fabrics; and Joan Fabrics of Lowell, which makes automotive upholstery. Such firms have several qualities in common. They all use old, low-cost mill buildings, they are very creative, they spend a lot of money on research and development, they use the very best machinery, and they have a high proportion of product output to labor input. Also, most of what they produce is made to order for their customers; it is not run off for inventory and selling in annual lines, as is the practice at the big standard goods mills in the South.

For most of its years, Quaker was a family business. Louis J. I. Symonds, a self-trained engineer and bookkeeper who had risen through the Depression and World War II to be the manager of a small company in Clinton, Massachusetts, set out on his own after the war. In 1946 he purchased some old looms to establish a family business in Pawtucket, Rhode Island, under the name of General Textile Mills. The initial arrangement called for a partner to be the salesman, for Louis to manage the plant, and for Louis's eldest son, Bernard, an imaginative Harvard graduate, to be the designer. Frieze was the specialty of the new firm. Frieze is a loop pile upholstery fabric whose origins lay in the Renaissance, when it was run off as a napped woolen fabric for coats. Initially the company was too small to do more than weave. It purchased its yarn and had its fabrics dyed by other companies. In these beginning years, also, it had no access to large furniture manufacturers. Instead, it serviced the needs of small furniture companies who themselves lacked the credit and purchasing power to deal with first-run suppliers.[26]

A year after it was founded, a small Philadelphia weaver of upholstery fabrics, Quaker Pile Fabric Company, purchased General Textile. The Philadelphia company's general manager, Harry Sovel, had been drawn to young Bernard's fabrics, and he was looking for a way to expand his own line. In the new arrangement he moved the sales office to New York City and sent his machinery to Pawtucket, where Louis Symonds was to tend the mill and his son to continue as designer.

In 1955, upon his graduation from Harvard, Alan Symonds, the younger son, an English literature major, joined the firm and began his sales apprenticeship under Harry Sovel. A time of turmoil soon followed. In 1957 Sovel died unexpectedly at the age of forty-eight. Thereupon the owner of the business, Oscar Leventhal, came out of retirement in Los Angeles to reorganize the firm. A kind of grandfather-grandson relationship sprang up between Leventhal and young Symonds. Leventhal, perhaps distrusting his own relatives who also worked in the New York office, put twenty-five-year-old Alan in charge of the business. He was to select the goods, set the prices, and handle the complaints.

More confusion followed. Louis Symonds died the next year so that Bernard was forced to take over his father's role, and he didn't like following orders from a brother in New York who was sixteen years his junior. At this point Leventhal sold his company to the two brothers. Bernard assumed the role of president, designer, and plant manager in Pawtucket, while Alan took charge of sales and did business out of New York City as Quaker Fabric. All during these years the firm remained small. It did $4–5 million worth of business each year but still had no access to the large manufacturers.

The first big break came in 1962–63. Because of Leventhal's Los Angeles residence, Quaker had a fine salesman and good connections there. In the late 1950s and early 1960s a woolen worsted fabric, a sort of heavy hopsack finished in neutral colors, captured the fashion in expensive furniture covering. The California salesman sent in a sample of this material, asking Alan if he could find an inexpensive way to imitate it. Just then Quaker was purchasing its yarn from a linen spinning company in Pennsylvania. They were able to make a good imitation on their machines using a rayon acetate mix. Bernard Symonds was in France on his honeymoon at the time. Perhaps because of his absence, the trial loom at Quaker was set up incorrectly, but by happy accident, the mistake allowed the loom to produce a fine imitation of the expensive woolen material. This successful imitation brought the big manufacturers to Quaker's door. Companies like La-Z-Boy, Sears, Steelcase, and Brookline placed large orders. Soon the boys needed sixty thousand pounds of yarn each week, and the business more than doubled to $10–15 million per year. When Bernard returned, the brothers purchased their own spinning plant, and they began to look for a large building where they might concentrate all their operations. Two years later when Bernard died at the age of forty-eight, Alan, then thirty-two, became the sole manager of the family's business.

In 1965 Fall River was a ghost town, abandoned by most of its textile mills and clothing manufacturers. Following extended negotiations, Quaker purchased one million square feet of old mill buildings for $1 per square foot; after a year of repairs it moved its operations to the new Fall River site next to the harbor, where it still remains. In the midst of all these changes Alan Symonds's wife died in 1966, leaving him with three small children to raise. He later remarried an anthropology professor at Brown University who had three children herself. They subsequently had one child together and raised their family of seven.

The second break grew out of Bernard's earlier initiatives. He had been experimenting with a DuPont product, Taslan. Here a cheap filament was transformed into a bulky yarn by blowing and fixing other fibers onto the core filament. Alan had hired the former manager of Stevens Linen, Bob Mostertz, to assume Bernard's role. Mostertz followed up the Taslan development by going to Ireland to purchase linen-spinning machines to spin yarn-dyed polypropylene (olefin). This fiber, both hydrophobic and second only to nylon in durability, soon became a major upholstery category, and the core of Quaker's line.

The third break came in 1970–71, when Mostertz and Symonds heard that a Philadelphia firm that made beautiful chenille yarns was for sale by its aging owners. These men had adapted existing machines to spin their high-quality yarns. Quaker purchased the plant and moved it to Fall River. The chenilles have also been a big success.

The 1970s proved a difficult decade; sales were low during the oil crisis, and there were troubles too with the introduction of computer control of the business. By 1980 Quaker had recovered and was able to purchase new machinery once more. The 1980s, however, carried Quaker on the roller-coaster ride of finance capitalism. In 1982 a Leominster, Massachusetts, flocking company, Vertipile, took control of Quaker through a leveraged buyout. The new owner subsequently soon died, and Alan Symonds responded by purchasing the stock holdings of the estate. Yet times were difficult. The leveraged buyout left Quaker short of cash, and Vertipile itself proved to be a mediocre firm. In 1988 Quaker lost money, and the Vertipile board of directors considered putting the company up for sale once more.

Amidst these difficulties and confusions, an overseas business directed by Edward C. Johnson III entered Quaker's life. This newcomer was not the warm, fuzzy branch of Johnson's Fidelity mutual fund empire. Rather, it was an investment pool that specialized in forcing sales and mergers to realize quick cash profits. Fidelity International of Bermuda had been buying Quaker stock to the proportion of 20 percent of the outstanding shares on the hunch that the turmoil had depressed the share price well below the firm's sale value.[27] Fidelity put together a syndicate of Italian and New York investors and a Southern yarn company to purchase Quaker. Since the 1989 sale, Larry Liebenow, formerly of Nortex, has successfully managed Quaker Fabric and continued its role as a leader in the upholstery fabric industry. Today it has twenty-two hundred employees, eighteen hundred of whom are hourly staff who keep the mill running three shifts, seven days a week. Of these hands, 70 percent are Portuguese, Azorean immigrants or their descendants.[28] In this old industry, not only have the processes and products changed continually, but so have the sales practices. They now much more resemble the ways of high-technology companies like Boston Scientific and Parametric rather than the former style, which focused on the salesroom and the salesman's book of samples. Now there is a continuing cooperation between fabric maker and user. Members of the furniture companies' design departments come to Quaker, where together with Quaker designers they seek the most appropriate fabrics to stretch over the frames the manufacturers intend to offer in future lines. It is a kind of intraindustry teamwork that seems to be spreading through firms whose products can be readily adjusted and adapted to varying needs.

The Rockport Company is another survivor of an old and almost-gone New England industry, leather shoes. Leather shoemaking is an old and skilled craft whose origins in the Boston region lay in seventeenth-century Lynn. The industry prospered here, nourished by two sources. First, there was a continuing stream of mechanical inventions beginning in 1858 with the adaptation of the sewing machine to sew soles to uppers. Second, there was a plentiful supply of rural and immigrant labor to master the craft and tend the machines. By the end of World War I, the Boston region was ringed with shoe factories from Lynn and Beverly on the north to Marlborough on the west to Brockton and Middleboro on the south. Even the city of Boston had its large Plant and Stride-Rite shoe factories. As a labor-intensive industry it began to move south and overseas seeking cheap labor, and with the closing of immigration in the 1920s the skilled Boston labor force aged and was not replaced. Few young people wanted to master the craft or to spend a life working in a shoe factory. After World War II, as the industry thinned out, the related findings companies that made the laces, eyelets, and trimmings disappeared, thereby making it ever harder for those continuing here to compete. Today the region's shoe manufacturers, firms like Timberland and Bass, keep only a few plants in New Hampshire and Maine, where employment is hard to come by and wages are low.[29]

Rockport began as a sales idea, not a manufacturing one. It was a total contrast to the former local industry pattern. The old Boston shoe organization consisted of a regional hive of specialized factories that manufactured particular types of shoes to be sold to marketing companies. The manufacturers didn't have national brand names like Rockport or Walkover. Now the marketers of brand names make the production decisions.

In 1971 a father and son, Sol and Bruce Katz, people who had been in the shoe business for years, conceived of the idea of offering a line of comfortable informal leather shoes. The shoes themselves they would purchase overseas in places like Portugal, Italy, and Spain. They located their offices in Marlborough because it was a handy regional location, and because Marlborough had been for decades a shoe capital. At first the company enjoyed considerable success. In 1975 it had a burst of popularity with its "Walking Shoe," informal, brown leather, rubber-soled shoes for men and women. The overseas procurement kept the prices down, and the comfortable styles attracted a loyal following. Yet, as the years passed the restless waves of fashion eroded the business. Young people turned to athletic shoes fashioned out of cheap leather and all manner of cloth and plastic materials. Even old-timers could be seen giving up their traditional black and brown leather dress shoes for the comforts of track and field models.

In 1976 a very successful sports shoe marketer, Reebok of Stoughton, purchased Rockport to make it its brown leather division. Reebok was seeking a hedge against dark future days when track, basketball, and tennis footwear might no longer be dominant. For the Rockport staff the purchase brought access to a great deal of capital, and in the 1990s, fashion swerved anew: young people began to wear what the industry calls brown leather shoes once again. Even heavy boots are a fashion statement. Unfortunately, at the time of its sale to Reebok, Rockport had earned the debilitating reputation of being the shoes "your grandfather wears." [30]

In 1991 Reebok sent one of its most successful marketing executives to Rockport to revive the business. The problems were twofold: How to keep control of the manufacturing process? How to build outward from Rockport's stuffy fashion niche? The new CEO was Angel Martinez, then a thirty-three-year-old Cuban-born, Bronx-raised, All-American cross-country runner from the University of California at Davis. Martinez had been a rhetoric major at Davis, and after he graduated he continued running competitively. He also opened two shoe stores in Alameda and Mountain View, California, where he pioneered in offering multiple lines of high-tech shoes. Soon, however, managing amateur running clubs, raising a family, and tending the stores proved more than he could handle, so he sold the stores and became a West Coast sales representative for Reebok. [31]

His break came when he invented an athletic shoe for women. One day while watching his wife at her aerobics class he noticed that all the women were barefoot, even though some of the exercises were high impact. At the time, women's athletic shoes were just men's shoes made in smaller sizes. They were not designed for women's feet or for the angles of their hips and knees. Despite skepticism and reluctance at the home office, Martinez succeeded in getting trial pairs of special women's aerobic shoes made. As of 1995, thirty-five million pairs of such shoes had been sold, making Reebok a top athletic shoe maker, second only to Nike of Portland, Oregon. [32]

Martinez's design and manufacturing effort has been to introduce many of the techniques and materials of sport shoes into the making of brown leather shoes. The goal has been to keep the stability, wear, and general style of brown shoes while making them much lighter and more comfortable. For example, the Rockport standard businessman's wingtip shoe has been so lightened and reinforced in its interior that it was possible for a Rockport vice president to run the entire New York Marathon and finish in the front ranks wearing such a shoe. A conventional wingtip would have raised a hive of blisters well before the halfway mark. The company's line of boots has similarly been much lightened and made waterproof by using special molded shells inside the leather, and all the shoes, men's and women's, include foot beds to cradle the foot on top of its sole.

Brown shoes have always been fussy to make because flaws in the leather or the forming of the shoe stand out so clearly on the surface. Imperfections can't be hidden with white dye, as they can in an athletic shoe. Also, these new constructions have added to the complexity of shoemaking and intensified the need for quality control.

To deal with these problems Martinez has been reducing the number of his overseas suppliers and seeking long-term relationships. Currently Rockport has a dozen manufacturers in Portugal, Hungary, Spain, China, Thailand, Indonesia, and Brazil and will soon use a plant in Vietnam. In each of these countries there is a national Rockport inspector who hires a staff of plant inspectors. The plant inspectors, in turn, have the right to pull every fifth shoe off the production line for examination.

The Pro-Walker illustrates the company's problem. In 1997 Rockport introduced this popular shoe. So far, three million pairs have been sold. The manufacturing goal is to have less than 1 percent defective, that is, fewer than 30,000 pairs that can't be sold as first-quality shoes. Currently the control system has been holding the imperfection rate at 0.68 percent. Although the supervision is intrusive, the manufacturers benefit from the steady relationship, which enables them to plan. For instance, when Rockport wants to introduce a new shoe with a part leather, part plastic sole, the machine required may require a $3 million investment. Such innovations demand planning on both sides.

This overseas sourcing also makes the company vulnerable to criticism for supporting child labor and exploitative sweatshops. Rockport's inspectors are instructed to make the promise to customers of no child labor a truthful statement. Also, in 1998, Rockport's parent, Reebok, joined a number of shoe and apparel firms in proposing a system of independent inspectors for their overseas plants. Their agreements are still in debate about the demands of American unions that the standards include a local "living wage" as one of the measures. Also countries like China pose a special problem, because they forbid labor organization.[33]

The shoe business is a restless fashion business, so maintaining and enlarging Rockport's position is Martinez's principal responsibility. In the suburban Marlborough office building he has six hundred employees—sales, finance, marketing, and design staff. To be profitable this group must come up with two hits each year within its line of several dozen men's and women's shoes.

The basic decision has been to build on Rockport's established position of comfortable shoes. The shoes must be attractive and stylish, but they will not attempt to follow high fashion trends. There are no Rockport platform shoes for women, nor sharp pointed shoes for men, nor will the firm attempt stiletto heels should they return once more. As Martinez put it in a talk to the industry, the goal is not to steal design space from others but rather to add to what all the companies are doing by having something original that will encourage people to buy shoes.[34] Rockport's introductions are comfortable, light, semiformal.

The marketing theme has been "active comfort," with the line ranging from refined styles for office work to rugged outdoor walkers and boots to relaxed weekend styles. A campaign to create a global brand recognition and loyalty has been added to this marketing theme so that the firm will not be selling one style in Brazil, another in the United Kingdom, and a third in Italy. Rather, they intend to market the whole line internationally.

The product development process is an interactive one. Designers and craftsmen at Marlborough make model shoes, which are sent out as samples to leading retailers for comment. At the same time more samples are placed in Rockport's own outlets, its "concept stores." At these stores, in Boston, San Francisco, Newport, Rhode Island, King of Prussia, Pennsylvania, White Plains, and New York City, trained staff do careful fitting and offer foot massage. Here customer reactions to the shoes, even wear trials, are sought. After this pretesting, the list of proposed shoes is trimmed back to an established core of best-sellers and a few hopeful new additions. In a bonanza year the company will have a hit like its Pro-Walker.

It is impossible to guess the future of such a firm as Rockport. Right now it is a very skillful company that is carefully attending to all the branches of its business from the introduction of new manufacturing methods to careful marketing techniques. Like the Boston region as a whole, it has no special advantages except access to an abundance of capital. Its only resource is the energy, experience, and imagination of its staff and executives. It is, thus, a perfect metaphor for the entire economy of the region.

The businessmen interviewed here form a group that well represents the new Boston region. They are a mix of locally born and raised and newcomers. The immigrants came from Czechoslovakia, Russia, and Cuba, the out-of-towners from New York, New Jersey, and Pennsylvania. Ethnically they are Jews, Irish, and Anglos. Some came to study at the local colleges; most came seeking business opportunities for their talents.

With the exception of Lawrence Lasser, who has made a career within one established firm (Putnam Investments), all of the group are founders and managers of new businesses. Some of these firms represent the institutionalization of new inventions, others are new ways of carrying on an established line. What all the men share most is a concentrated consumer orientation. The manufacturers among them all do custom work, while the business services men are in and out of their customers' offices trying to match customer needs to fresh offerings. In this they seem a restless group, always seeking. For them there is no one right way, rather ever-shifting futures.

CHAPTER THREE

So You Want to Be a Yankee?

From the first Plymouth settlement of the 1620s, Yankees have been town people. Yankees, whether farmers, fishermen, or merchants, made their homes in towns, centered places with a cluster of churches, lodges, clubs, and sewing circles, their formal politics governed by the unique town meeting form of government. The farms themselves were small, the extent of most of the towns, small too, but the gossip was dense. The first settlers assigned all the land in the Boston city region to bounded towns; Boston town was only the most populous. Later, some of the biggest towns changed their form of government to be cities, but towns are the Yankee way, and settled Yankees live in cities as if they were small towns.[1]

A century and a half ago, by the mid-nineteenth century, Massachusetts had been transformed into a hive of small factory cities and mill villages. There was hardly a stream so small that it had not been dammed and harnessed to power a mill that fashioned something or other. There, amidst the clatter of machinery, the caricature of the Yankee was born, a product of a strong current of nostalgia for the times before mills, immigrants, steam engines, banks, and the cant of progress.

The first old-time Yankee was a taciturn, hardworking, ingenious tinkerer whose iconoclastic views often shocked his minister, but whose honesty and reliability made him a worthy husband and

Mechanics Lane, New Bedford

father and a loyal friend to any who could spare the time to penetrate the armor of his reticence. The wife was the more sociable member of the pair; hearty, capable, and ingenious like her husband, she could turn her hand to everything from infant care to town politics. You can read a fresh-minted version of such characters in Harriet Beecher Stowe's *Oldtown Folks* (1869).

By their plain living and integrity, these admirable fictions held a mirror up to the parade of awkward new Victorian wealth and fashion. In later years there appeared card after card of stage Yankees, acts that culminated in the radio comedian Fred Allen's burlesque of the Maine farmer, Titus Moody, and Moody's urban opposite, George Apley.[2] Even these days, coffeehouse humorists mock our foibles with dialogues of such imagined antiques.

The bite of this humor draws upon more than the contrast between contemporary foolishness and some old-fashioned clearsightedness. These are stories of lost community, of villages and neighborhoods where people knew each other. The audience's wish for community thus reinforces their pleasure in commonsensical humor.

Thereby the New England town remains a wellspring of community in the Boston region because these bounded municipalities of a few square miles provide a focus for people who care about community life, a place where the willing can find a comfortable role for themselves. We have long since left behind the days when to be a Yankee required that you not be a Catholic, a Jew, an African American, or a recent immigrant. World War II and the civil rights movement put an end to that sort of village exclusion. Now the town tradition flourishes among us because it continues to be relived and reimagined.

One strong company of contemporary Yankees is recruited from the locals, folks who were born and raised in a town and who have continued to live out their lives in their birthplace. These are people who by following a life course within one town or municipality lend their personal character to the meaning of that place. No one is a more settled townsman than Buzzy Bartone of Natick. Everyone at the Main Street coffee shop knows Buzzy. Like the old Natick farmers who preceded him, Buzzy has kept his feet firmly planted on the ground so that he could make step-by-step progress through life to an admirable old age. His parents immigrated from a village sixty miles beyond Naples, Italy. There were two boys and a girl, and the Bartones spoke Italian in their home. The father, a mason, started a landscaping business, laying up stone walls, setting out driveways, planting and tending lawns, shrubs, and trees. Buzzy and his older brother helped out while they were schoolchildren. "We had to," Buzzy said. He was born during the Great Depression, in 1934.

A popular young man, he played baseball and basketball for Natick High School, and later basketball for a Veterans of Foreign Wars team. His father died a few years after Buzzy's graduation, so for the next decade he worked for his brother, who took over the landscaping business. The firm was busy enough; it had a good list of clients that included owners of big houses in nearby Wellesley.

Buzzy is self-taught, a follower of that deep American tradition of little schooling and lots of lifetime learning. He picked up his gardening skills from watching his brother, but also from courses and books. He attended two-day seminars at Massachusetts Bay Community College and short courses at Russell's Garden Center, nearby, and he listened faithfully to a Saturday morning radio expert. After he married, in 1973, he asked his wife to give him garden books for Christmas. He became a skilled gardener, "the impatient and intense" member of the Bartone team. The brother, however, wasn't good at the business side of the work. He was content to take home a day's pay. "He was too conscientious; he never should have been in business," Buzzy recalls. Rather than quarrel with his brother, however, Buzzy got a copy of the Red Book from a friend, passed the exam, and joined the Natick Fire Department. From 1965 to 1993 he worked as a fireman and helped his brother periodically during his days off.

In 1973 he purchased his present house on Franconia Avenue, off Main Street, the first single house he had ever lived in. The couple raised a son and a daughter, both of whom went to the University of Massachusetts, in Amherst. Mrs. Bartone works as an assistant to the business manager of the Rivers School, a preparatory school in nearby Weston. When his brother died in 1986, Buzzy took up singing in the choir at St. Patrick's. Then, a few years later, he retired from the fire department and started his own landscaping business with a couple of dozen clients. He doesn't own a plow or any heavy equipment, but he enjoys his gardens and his clients, even to the extent of shopping for and looking after an old Italian widow whose family has moved to Florida. Winters he cleans his friend's apartment buildings. The town of Natick, like many Boston towns, is now trying to rebuild its old town center in the wake of its destruction by giant shopping malls on the nearby highway (State Route 9). More important than new buildings, people like Buzzy, through their services, long residence, and good-natured address create the centered community the town restorers are seeking.[3]

Carol Pimentel seems as anchored to New Bedford as any old farmer or fisherman. New Bedford is a considerable place, in fact a city of 100,000 residents, but Carol lives within it like the best of Yankee townsmen. Now director of Internal Audit for nearby University of Massachusetts at Dartmouth, Carol knows just about everybody in New Bedford, and they seem to know her too. Today she lives the modern professional woman's life, sharing a two-family house with her mother on Cottage Street, on New Bedford's comfortable West Side. It has, however, been a long progress, helped along by many.

Carol's maternal grandfather came to New Bedford as a whaleman in the second decade of the twentieth century. Her parents had little time for schooling; her mother made it through the eighth grade, her father only the fourth. Carol's memory is that her father worked himself out with overwork, on the first shift at Goodyear Tire and Rubber and then evenings tending a small Cape Verdean restaurant he owned. After the father died, her mother worked as a custodian in a garment factory and later as a cleaning lady.

Carol was born on Christmas Day in 1946, the third of seven children, two boys and five girls. One brother has since died; all the rest live in and around New Bedford, and many come together on Saturdays. At Thanksgiving and Christmas the whole tribe gathers with their husbands, wives, and children. Carol has remained single, and within the family she functions as telephone central. In public life, however, she has been the pioneer, out in front over and over again.

Carol did not begin as a leader. In high school she did the teenager's jobs of babysitting and housecleaning. After graduating from high school she worked the first year in a pajama factory and then found a job as a bank teller. Here, she thought, she had finally secured a safe, steady place for a woman. The excitement and possibilities of the 1960s, however, carried her on. One day a local civil rights worker, Duncan Dottin, said to her, "You don't want to be a bank teller all your life." He persuaded her to go on to college and to put her special talents to work. Carol is that rare person who likes both numbers and people. It was then, in the late 1960s, that her career took off, carrying her into the world of modern professionals.

She majored in accounting at the nearby University of Massachusetts campus. She played basketball and rose to be captain of the team. The tennis coach taught her to play tennis, and within a year she had made the team. Ever since she has enjoyed being a tennis player. Hers is an energetic life that grew out of business and politics. After graduating in 1972 she went on to take a master's degree in education administration at Boston University. At that moment she dreamed of a new life in California. She went out there looking for a job, but when her brother called to tell her that a big real estate development firm had an opening for an accountant, she returned. The Peabody Properties Corporation was then working on federally funded projects, and it needed to comply with the Affirmative Action regulations. Carol was the first black woman in their administrative office. From 1977 to 1987 she commuted from New Bedford to Braintree, where the corporate offices were located.

Meanwhile a descendant of an old New Bedford family, John Bullard, a Harvard-trained city planner, returned to his hometown to run for mayor with the goal of stopping the city's urban renewal projects, which were tearing out the best of the old city. Elected in 1987, Bullard recruited Pimentel to join his staff as city auditor, a first again. From the auditor's office she soon moved to be director of Community Development, the office that managed all the federal funds for community service and housing. After six constructive and exciting years, Mayor Bullard was defeated by a group that saw their chance in the Reagan backlash to run on a low-tax campaign. Mayor Bullard was particularly vulnerable at that time because he had undertaken a very necessary, but very expensive, step to build a sewage treatment plant to reduce the pollution of New Bedford Harbor.

For ten scary months Carol found herself out of work. Finally she landed a job as an auditor in the president's office at the University of Massachusetts. There, as one member of its special task force to evaluate the condition of the University of Massachusetts campus at Dartmouth, she was hired by the incoming campus chancellor. "There is something that keeps me here in New Bedford," Carol said.

A good deal of that something must be the Cape Verdeans of New Bedford. For years Carol ran the annual Cape Verdean Bike Ride and Independence Day Picnic, which takes place on July 5. Cyclists pedal an eighteen-mile course to a finish on the south side at Hazelwood Park, where they join their families for a picnic and large celebration. In addition, Carol has been invited to join many community boards, including that of the Boys and Girls Club, an institution that is desperately needed in New Bedford because it is a depressed mill and fishing town suffering high unemployment. Like others in New Bedford and Cape Cod, Carol thinks that for young people to master a skill they must at least go to the central Boston area for training or to attend college. Perhaps later, when business picks up, they can return to find good jobs. If they stay in the neighborhoods, however, they will encounter high school dropouts, unemployment, drugs, and trouble.

You might guess that Carol's political days are not finished, but she is very busy, politics or no, as a community person. Like others she is disappointed that the twenty-five to thirty-five-year-olds are not coming forward. They seem not to be aware of civil rights as a pressing and ongoing issue. Carol observes, "They are just doing their personal lives." Yet, for herself, "being single, I have a lot of opportunities to help people."[4]

There are many Yankees like Buzzy and Carol who invent and nourish community life in the region's towns and cities. Roger Woods of Abington repeated the common pattern of graduating from high school as a sports star, then becoming a local real estate man and town selectman.[5] Less often recognized are the abundant innovations of newcomers who adopt the town they settle in. A good estimate would guess that at least half of the community institutions in any Boston city or town are managed and staffed by out-of-towners who have settled in from elsewhere. Mary Allor, an often-moved-about corporate wife, brought to Hopkinton her organizing skills to help establish a much-needed and popular Newcomer's Club in that growing suburban town.[6] Larry Walsh of Everett is an outbound commuter who edits a weekly paper for the town of Woburn, where he gives to that mobile population a sense of centeredness.[7] Jay Scott, an architecture graduate of the Massachusetts Institute of Technology, moved to one of Boston's beleaguered Dorchester neighborhoods. She commenced her organizing there by opening her yard to the neighborhood children so they could play in a safe place.[8] Ed and Mary Frances O'Brien are newcomers to Boston who have become park restorers and community rebuilders in Mattapan, a Boston section of poor Caribbean immigrants and long-settled Bostonians.[9] Susan Naimark of Jamaica Plain long worked to foster Boston's urban gardens and later turned to housing issues.[10] All such newcomers to the city of Boston are restoring communities where poverty and frequent turnover of residents can leave city dwellers feeling isolated and helpless.

Those who work directly upon a town's sense of itself also nourish its traditions. Karin Gertsch of Essex and her husband are devoted town meeting attenders. He, a former farmer turned landscaper, is the son of an immigrant Swiss plant propagator. She is an army child, the daughter of a German war bride and a career tank officer. After raising two children herself, and years of volunteering at the library and the hospital, she began to research the history of the world around her. She discovered three hundred books about Cape Ann. She also realized that the area was a prime tourist destination, popular with German tourists too, so she wrote down her appreciation in a guidebook, *Cape Ann and Vicinity* (1997). Next she began work on a guide to Salem and surroundings.[11] Karilyn Crockett and Denise Thomas, young Yale graduates, have worked up a multicultural tour of the South End and Roxbury sections of Boston, which they aptly named MYTOWN. Summers they train high school students to be guides.[12] In Natick, Lynda Simkins has transformed a former juvenile delinquency program into a vital organic farm that trains fourteen-year-olds in farming and work skills and simultaneously furnishes useful work to Down's syndrome children and women from a nearby detoxification center.[13]

A disproportionate number of these town dwellers and town makers are women. For instance, Elizabeth Berg is a successful novelist who has settled in Natick. Raised as an army child, she lived just about everywhere. She trained and worked as a nurse, married a physicist, had two daughters, and lived with her family in Chicago and several Boston towns. In 1985 she won an essay contest and ever since has been writing. Divorced in 1996, she moved close to Natick's old town green.

In her ways of living and in her novels Elizabeth Berg transforms a spread-out post–World War II tract and mall suburb into a centered town. Her fictional characters neighbor in and out of each other's houses (*Range of Motion*, 1995). In real life, when she is not a traveling author, she stops at Ed's Place with her *Times* and her *Globe* for breakfast and a chat with the waitress. When you speak with her you can hear her populate her town with characters. In her mind and in her books she has already revived the old town center even before the old brick blocks have been refurbished and the empty storefronts reoccupied.[14]

There is nothing new about this behavior. William Dean Howells settled in Boston and Belmont from Columbus, Ohio. Once here he wrote novels and stories that gave Boston its 1890s reputation. The reading public so enjoyed his charming and modest-living Boston couple, the Marches, that he wrote three volumes to satisfy the demand. Americans today regard Robert Frost, a Californian transferred to Lawrence, as the quintessential Yankee poet, an explorer of the darker side of our stone walls and the encroaching city and forest. For many high school students Yankee means *Ethan Frome*, a tale of an archetypal Yankee village. The village and its heroine were the invention of a New York and Newport society lady. John Updike, our leading novelist today, is a Pennsylvanian. In all this writing the local community, whether it be city, farm town, or suburb, is a presence, a defining force with which the characters must contend. Moreover, all these Yankee authors write with a strong moral edge as if by adopting this place to be their home they felt some emanations of the anxieties of the Puritans percolating through the soil beneath their feet.

Caring about a region does not make its politics any easier. In fact, politics in the cities and towns of the Boston region are as difficult as they are everywhere else in the United States. We are a diverse people, and consensus comes hard. Although an occasional hot topic, like the tearing down of houses to build a highway or a sharp rise in taxes or the firing of a popular schoolteacher or superintendent, will turn out a crowd, most of the time the problem with local politics is ignorance and apathy. In suburban Halifax no one came forward in 1998 to fill either a vacancy on the school board or one on the board of selectmen. In affluent Duxbury, only 6 percent of the voters turned out at the 1997 local election.[15] Duxbury tries to counteract apathy by holding its town meeting in March, when the weather is nasty. It serves high-quality catered food and offers babysitting. If the warrant is a long one the meetings run from Saturday to Monday and Tuesday, but not into the night. Hingham holds no Saturday town meetings in deference to its Jewish population.[16]

The open town meeting, in which every voter is a member, can be a long and wearing experience with sessions lasting all day and late into the night. Some towns have experimented with secret ballots so that people will not be embarrassed by showing their approval or disapproval to their neighbors sitting close by. The consequence of this reform has been a rash of votes against all new initiatives. Indeed, some commentators see the secret ballot innovation to be the sinister work of a New Hampshire antitax organization. Other towns have experimented with separate school and town business meetings, but the division has not worked well either. Turnout fell for both sessions.[17]

Lack of voter attentiveness can ferment into corruption, or at least what Boss Plunkett of New York City once called "honest graft," sweet deals for insiders in the know.[18] The South Shore town of Weymouth, the site of the very first town meeting (1624), in 1999 voted for a mayor and city council form of government because of corruption in town offices. Now a town of fifty-five thousand and seventeen hundred municipal employees, the voters hoped that representation by professional politicians might give them a more reliable town management.[19]

Framingham, however, the region's largest town (population 65,000), voted to keep its representative town meeting. In 1998 a group of reformers proposed a city charter in the hope of obtaining what they called more professional management. The voters rejected the proposal, three to one. The most powerful argument against the change addressed the openness of elections. To run as a town meeting representative, a person need only print up a few cards and perhaps a few signs to put on supporters' lawns. By contrast, candidates spend thousands of dollars to win city council and mayoral seats. In 1998 the man elected to be mayor of Newton (83,000 residents) spent $150,000. Framingham will continue as one of the three hundred Massachusetts cities and towns that employ the town meeting form.[20]

Apathy, taxes, fraud, good management, and the need for new projects will never disappear from local government and local politics no matter what happens to the town meeting as a form of government. What is essential, and what is most likely to preserve the town meeting form, are people who enjoy being part of their communities and who care enough to take some responsibility for them.

Selectman William McDevitt is such a person. He has been a resident of the Boston region town of Pelham, New Hampshire, for twenty-eight years. Here he and his wife, Joyce, have raised their seven children. He has served on many town committees, and for the past eight years as a selectman. Like many Yankee townsmen, he came to Pelham from somewhere else.

He was born in Norristown, Pennsylvania, during World War II while his father, an insurance man for John Hancock Life Insurance Company, was in the military. Thereafter the family moved about the Philadelphia area, to Pittsburgh, then Chicago, finally settling in Harrisburg, Pennsylvania. It was there, in high school, that he met Joyce. He then went on to study and graduate from St. Joseph's College in Philadelphia and joined John Hancock. Bill and Joyce married in 1965, moved to Chicago, and began having babies. After a number of assignments in the Chicago area, Bill was brought back to the home office in Boston in 1969, where he now does customer service and program quality supervision.

His associates at John Hancock warned him not to move to the south side of Boston because there was too much traffic on the Southeast Expressway (I-93). Instead, they said, look for a house to the north. "It's cheap up there, the taxes are low, and there's no one there." Bill found a small new house in Nashua, New Hampshire, but it proved too small for his growing family. Later on, when he learned that the builder of his house was developing a subdivision in Pelham, he purchased his present house there.

The McDevitts have been in Pelham since 1972. It is a small country town nestled between two highways, U.S. 3 and I-93, a typical place on the far edge of the Boston city region. At the crossroads of the town stand two churches, the library, the town offices, and a small store. There are no sidewalks, no bus or train service. Formerly a one-horse rural town, it is now a bedroom town of ten thousand inhabitants, and perhaps as many cars. Unfortunately, the McDevitts could afford but one car for the first twelve years of their life in Pelham. Bill needed it for a 55–75-minute commute to Copley Square in Boston. This left Joyce and the seven children in a new subdivision of fifty houses scatted on acre-and-a-half lots in the woods. Joyce traded favors with the other mothers nearby, and in emergencies relied on the police. When one daughter's face ballooned up from a wasp bite, she called the police. The cruiser came, took the child to the hospital, waited there, stopped off at the pharmacy for the drugs, and returned with the child.

Bill and Joyce had no time for the PTA, but all the children went through the Pelham schools, and most are now scattered about nearby. For many years Joyce and the children proved to be essential supports for Bill's election campaigns. Joyce stands at the polls with him each election year to greet all her friends and acquaintances, and, as Bill put it, each of his children had fifteen friends.

In 1972, the year the family acquired two cars, Bill ran for library trustee. He remembered how important the escape to the library had been to him as a child. Defeated in his first try, he ran again and was elected in 1974 and subsequently served for thirteen years. The role is an important one, since in New Hampshire there is no state aid for libraries; they must depend on the annual appropriations of the town meeting, gifts, and book sales. Bill's service at the library led to other town committees and a reputation as someone who was willing to work on town affairs.

In 1992, upon the retirement of two selectmen, he ran successfully for a seat on the Board of Selectmen. The year coincided with the bottom of the Reagan-Bush depression, a time when the nearby high-tech firms, Raytheon, Digital, Sanders, and Wang, were laying off employees. Many townspeople were overextended in their mortgages, and empty storefronts appeared in the town's strip mall on the Dracut-Windham road (Route 38). Real estate prices fell for both single-family homes and condominiums. There was much pain and suffering. Unfortunately, the selectmen could do little. Some called for building a town water and sewer system as a way to make jobs, but such an effort far exceeded the resources of the town, especially since its tax base had declined with the real estate market. Moreover, the project itself lacked justification. Pelham has lots of good water; it sits on one of New Hampshire's largest aquifers. If, in the future, intense urbanization should result in heavy pumping of the aquifer, as has happened along the Charles River, then Pelham's private wells and septic systems will recharge the aquifer and protect the water resources of the town.

In his years as selectman Bill has learned a great deal about the essential ingredients for a successful town. There are poor families in Pelham, as in every other town in the Boston city region. The town is these families' first resource before they can qualify for state aid, and also their resource for unusual expenses. For example, a man needed a new pair of eyeglasses; the town clerk wrote him a check.

Pelham spent $50,000 in 1997 on such help. There is a food pantry in a house owned by St. Patrick's church, and the Congregational church cooperates in serving it. Drugs are not a problem, but, of course, they could become so. The police chief is worried about daytime robberies, since so many families are out of their houses working. The chief commutes across the Boston region to Pelham from Quincy. The selectmen would like him to settle in town, like the other officers. The police station is too small; so is the library. The schools are overcrowded. In New Hampshire all these improvements must be financed by the town taxes on property.

Out of such issues the politics of the town reveal themselves. Race is not an issue. There are a few African American families in town, and a Pentecostal church on the road to Salem, New Hampshire, serves a multitown congregation. Black versus white is not an axis of conflict. Rather, Pelham divides as towns always do between those who want improved services and facilities and those who want to save and to cut taxes. Pelham is also divided by political groupings. The new prosperous white-collar families are so far not participating in town affairs. Both parents are commuting to jobs all over the region; they have one or two children; and when they are at home they want to spend time with their children, not doing community work. There is also a strong radical antigovernment group whose ideology goes beyond saving taxes. Bill calls these folks the "Live Free or Die" people, borrowing the state slogan. They are people who wish to dismantle the land-use controls that have been put in place during the past thirty years, do home schooling, and sharply cut back on government activities.

Bill's experience teaches him otherwise. The sort of towns that people admire throughout the Boston region, towns like Peterborough, New Hampshire, Rockport, Natick, Brookline, and Duxbury, are all pleasant places to live because of the thick webs of community organizations. They do not depend alone on the wisdom and resources of the selectmen, who are, after all, part-time volunteers

District	Percentage	District	Percentage
Lincoln	22.4	Marblehead	16.7
Boston	21.5	Needham	16.4
Somerville	20.0	Dracut	15.9
Wellesley	18.6	Beverly	15.8
Arlington	17.1	Malden	15.7
Weymouth	16.9	Quincy	15.1
Newton	16.8		

whose main jobs lie elsewhere.[21] Instead, the many organizations for schools, charity, recreation, and the arts enrich the life of the town.

Beneath the ideal of a highly reticulated community rests the inescapable fact that cities and towns abide with two polarities: property and schools. At the one end stand the necessities and conflicts over municipal services, assessments, zoning, and new development. At the other end stand the children, teachers, and schools. Within the Massachusetts part of the Boston city region there are 156 school districts. Most have less than 10 percent of their children attending private schools. Thirty-eight wealthy suburbs and old cities and suburbs with well-developed parochial systems have more than 10 percent outside (table 2).[22]

The proportion of children in private schools does not predict the quality of the local public schools, nor does these children's outside attendance substantially reduce the educational budgets of their municipalities. The needs and the ambitions of the various public schools do not respond to such a simple accounting. Yet public education stands in frequent conflict with the property side of the ledger. Typically cities and towns spend about 60 percent of their annual budget on education.

Near Pelham, in Derry, New Hampshire, these financial tensions display themselves in dramatic opposition. Here a local high school teacher and parent of two children, Michael Arrato Gavrish, is forced to spend a great deal of his time and effort in persuading his fellow citizens that well-financed public schools are essential. For the past few years Derry's elementary schools (grades 1–8) have been suffering from a taxpayer revolt and roller-coaster budgets. Derry is New Hampshire's fourth largest town (population 30,000), thanks to a new highway (Interstate 93) and boom times in the 1980s. Condominium clusters and streets of singles and side-by-side doubles sprouted throughout the town. Then, as in Pelham, depression struck, the housing market collapsed, and buyers could not be found.

Because of New Hampshire's peculiar politics, the depression bit more sharply here than in the Massachusetts segments of the Boston region. New Hampshire lacks both sales and income taxes, so all the town services must rest on the local property tax. This concentrated tax burden weighed especially heavily when the real estate market grew stagnant. At the same time, a lawsuit over assessments mandated that a reduction be made for condominiums and that single-family homes be taxed more. The decision sparked a taxpayer revolt. School budgets then shrank, teachers and programs were cut, and soon some families with money removed their children to private schools.

Here, as elsewhere, tax politics conceal many conflicts. The old oppose the young families with children. Those holding tracts of open land for future development want their taxes kept down while they wait. The newcomers want improved services now. Many Derry residents work in Massachusetts, where they must pay an income tax on their earnings there. For these, the high property tax seems an unusual burden. The radicals in town wish to sharply cut back

Sunshine Condominiums, Derry, N.H.

Bank's Mobile Homes, Second Lane, Derry, N.H.

all government. Some propose home schooling; others, charter schools and vouchers to replace the existing public schools. Still others are disaffected because they feel the town has lost the power to govern its own schools owing to the many state and federal mandates that set standards without contributing the bulk of the money. In New Hampshire, as throughout the nation, the state government is struggling to meet its constitutional obligations for equal treatment by devising new taxes to equalize town educational resources. At the moment, Derry and New Hampshire students do well on the California Tests, which rank pupils but do not measure student ability by absolute criteria. Gavrish fears the outcome of the new state criterion tests.

Gavrish himself is caught in the middle of considerable cultural and symbolic confusion. He teaches at an institution whose mode of governance precedes the creation of public schools. He teaches U.S. history to juniors and seniors at Derry's Pinkerton Academy (founded 1814). Pinkerton is one of a few survivors of an old New England tradition, the town academy that teaches all who are sent. In the eighteenth and early nineteenth centuries, well-to-do gentlemen established many such schools for their towns. Then, in later years most towns switched to publicly controlled schools. Many academies languished, while a few transformed themselves into private preparatory schools with high tuition charges. Phillips Academy in Andover and its enfolded sister institution, Abbott Academy for Girls, is such an altered academy.

Pinkerton continues in the original form. Its board of trustees, filled by cooptation, receives payments from the town of Derry and a few nearby towns. In return, the school gives a high school education to all. It is thus a public school under private management. As a result it enjoys a steady revenue, is well managed, has access to trustee funds, and is able to raise additional funds from its alumni and the community.

New Hampshire's aggressive marketing of itself adds to the cultural and symbolic confusions swirling around school advocate Gavrish. New Hampshire tells itself and its visitors that it is a place of pastoral small towns set next to beautiful lakes or with mountain backdrops. For most of Derry's families, however, the actualities of their lives and jobs are involved with the businesses of the northern edge of the Boston city region, not farms, lakes, or mountains.[23]

The conflicts and confusions of New Hampshire are not limited to that edge of the Boston city region but appear throughout. Although Massachusetts bears a proud educational history and enjoys an extraordinary gathering of schools, colleges, and universities, its residents are currently unhappy with their public schools. In a 1998 poll, 52 percent of the respondents said they would transfer their children to private schools, if they could afford the tuition.[24] Everywhere the chatter is of vouchers, charter schools, religious schools, and private schools. In 1998 half of the Massachusetts children failed the new state criterion tests,[25] perhaps an intended result, since the test advocates wished to press for new goals for the state's students. School taxes continue to rise.

The contrast between the community skills and the school skills of Yankee townspeople, between their town management and their school imagination, is extraordinary. It is a contrast that can only be wondered at. For the town they manage ongoing conflicts and find compromises. Every town has volunteers for a wide range of activities, from sports to arts and crafts and to caregiving. Many town dwellers invent new ways and fresh institutions. When we look at Yankees in their roles as school parents and voters, however, the region seems deeply mired in stale routine or narrow bickering over mistakes and innovations.

The basic social structure of the region's elementary and middle schools (K–8) is extraordinarily uniform and in stark contrast to both the private schools and the workplaces of the adults. There are 1,009 public elementary and middle schools in the Boston city region. Scattered among them are 225 private schools, religious and secular. The most common size for public schools is 300–400 students. Forty-two percent of the public schools have 400 pupils or fewer, but 42 percent of the private schools have 200 or fewer. There are as well many public schools with more than 700 pupils, but very few such big private ones.[26]

The differing size distribution provokes curiosity. The varying sizes of the public schools do not correlate with the sizes of the towns and cities, nor with the amount that is spent per pupil, nor with the proportion of a town's students attending private schools. All these aspects of local education have their own particular histories and do not determine school size. For example, the wealthy and educationally ambitious suburb of Bedford (population 13,000) has 400-pupil schools. Next door, Lexington (population 29,000) has 400 and 500. Fall River, by contrast, a hard-pressed old mill city (population 93,000), has many 200-pupil schools.

Does the size of the children's schools matter? If so, how? Surely most of human life is social, and most of what we know and care about is knowledge about how to live among our fellow humans. Surely we want our children to learn the manners and social skills of our communities. Could it be that big schools are a conscious community effort to teach children about life in big institutions? But the adult world is so unlike these schools. Most of the adults in Massachusetts do not work in institutions as large as their children's schools. The average number of employees in manufacturing establishments in 1992 was 47; the average number in retail, 7.4; the average in services, 2.2.[27]

Could it be that the teachers and masters who run the smaller private schools know something about community that the public school boards do not? Perhaps. Do you want your children's classmates and all the teachers in the school to know your child's name? Sociological studies suggest that 150 to 200 is the largest gathering of people in which it is possible for everyone to know everyone else's name. The size of a company in a modern army ranges from

130 to 225. In business, when a firm grows larger than about 120, communication via paper or e-mail replaces face-to-face and telephone exchanges.[28]

Oftentimes when confronted by curious and surprising results it is best to stop reading the computer printouts and instead to pay a visit to the people who do the work. An easy conversation with Frank Gersony, a guidance counselor at Wakefield's Galvin Middle School, soon touched upon school culture, particularly the consumer wars now relentlessly pressed by national marketing and suffered by children, teachers, and parents. "This year the kids won't buy anything that doesn't have a logo," Frank said. "The other night at the parent-teachers meeting, a group of parents demanded that the school require uniforms. They were tired of buying a stream of clothes for their daughters and expensive outfits for their sons." The school decided to poll the parents to gauge the parents' desires.

Wakefield (population 25,000) is a comfortable suburb on the north side of the region, a former mill town turned commuter home. Like its middle school, the town has few very poor, few new immigrants, and few African Americans. Its population is well-established American, with an Italian flavor. Set at the end of a still-active Main Street, Galvin occupies the former high school buildings. Built in the 1950s, it is a spread-out two-story structure with well-lighted classrooms and long corridors of gray lockers and shiny yellow tile. A large school, 1,100 pupils in grades 5–8, it tries, as many middle schools do, to make some community for its teachers and students by dividing the grades into teams. For example, the eighth grade is split into two teams of 140 students. Each team is assigned a cluster of five teachers who instruct and follow the team's pupils. Galvin is also trying to do its best by the extraordinary variety of knowledge and learning skills that any public school contains. One period every day is set aside for remedial work and consultations among the teachers and pupils, and the school is exploring ways to make use of Howard Gardner's hypothesis of alternative kinds of intelligence (*Frames of Mind*, 1983). Wakefield and this school are also very strong in music, so Galvin offers an ambitious music program of band, orchestra, and chorus, both in school and after school. Here, as elsewhere in the region, money is always a problem. The school is popular—89 percent of its graduates go on to Wakefield High, but it is not so popular that the taxpayers are generous at town meeting time when they vote new budgets and new buildings.

In such a settled suburban school you might laugh at the clothing war as a passing folly, but it is one of this year's symptoms of the two cultures of a large school of ten- to fourteen-year-olds. Gersony went on to say, "The kids need definite guidelines in school. The kids want boundaries, even though they are in rebellion and are often being contrary." As everywhere, the middle school children of Wakefield lack experience. They have yet to become skilled community builders on their own.[29]

Lynne Nivica has taught English for the past dozen years at Norton Middle School. Norton is a small, almost rural town (population 14,000) on the Rhode Island edge of the region. It is just now experiencing the growing pains that follow upon new highway installations. Last year Norton opened a new middle school. Not only are its 600 children divided into three teams but the new building is partitioned to make a separate school place for each team. Ms. Nivica teaches creative writing, poetry, and expository writing to sixth-, seventh-, and eighth-graders. Often she selects a current topic as a writing assignment. In one such she gave out a news clip of student culture in an Illinois school. A particularly talented student, Sarah McGinty, wrote:

Children today are no different than the children of yesterday. But now, in the nineties, we can find more ways to display our petty rages and hates. We mock those who are smarter, who are stupider, who are poorer, and even those who are richer, only, we do it behind their backs. We step on those who are already down to keep them there, and we pull frequently at those who are on top to make them fall. Our weapons of choice are money, popularity (which has a great deal to do with money, and the next thing) and appearance. . . . We all believe, to some extent, that the top, meaning the top of the adolescent social structure, guarantees not happiness, but *safety*. (Author's emphasis)

The state criterion exams (Massachusetts Comprehensive Assessment System) are not forcing Lynne Nivica and her students to change their ways. The examinations test writing; she teaches writing.[30]

In Wakefield and Norton the consumer wars set off painful daily skirmishes from which most children and adults recover. Not so in places where poverty turns marketing into harassment and where possessions, and fantasies of possessions, isolate children from adults they might trust. Suzanne Belanger teaches sixth grade at Arnone School, a large (800 pupils) elementary school (grades 1–6) in Brockton. Brockton is an old shoe city (population 93,000) that has lost its former industries and is struggling to find a satisfactory niche in the new regional economy. Arnone School serves a poor inner-city neighborhood on the west side of the old downtown. Ninety-five percent of its children qualify for subsidized breakfast and lunch. Most are children of native poor, not immigrants. In her sixth grade, race does not separate the children. The kids seek to hang out with the big boys and girls, and with the youngsters with forceful personalities.

The children's problem, and the school's problem, is poverty. "An intact family is a rarity. Many mothers lack parenting skills," Belanger observes. "Some have no sense that they should put their child first. Many mothers and daughters lack self-esteem. They know that when they get pregnant the fathers disappear. Yet they get pregnant because they want someone, a baby, to love them."

And the commercially promoted class culture weighs upon the children: "Some of the kids are very mean to each other," Belanger continues. "They tease each other about whose parents are unemployed, who is on welfare, who wears what logo, who has the right sneakers. They are very possession, very property oriented." These attitudes and behaviors are those of "kids without confidence who are putting each other down."

Arnone is not all bad news. In each year's classes Belanger can sense which children are going to make it on through high school and to a successful adulthood. "It's mysterious," she says. "The successful ones may lack parents and are very much on their own. If they are going to get up in the morning to go to school, their alarm clock has to ring. Mother is asleep. If they are to do homework, they often do so without encouragement at home. But these children read, they are in the advanced programs, they're going on."

Suzanne Belanger previously taught for two years at a very remarkable small Boston school for poor children, Nativity Prep. It is a school designed to advance children through intensive schooling. Belanger shares that goal. Her goal at Arnone is "to help my children do better than their parents." She says it is difficult to do much in a school of 800 because it so concentrates the problems of the town, but she thinks she can "convert a few each year." Her method is to let her children "experience success, earned success, not given success." She is devoted to her school and her children, even the troublemakers. Yet, neither Brockton nor the Commonwealth of Massachusetts is willing to spend the money to summon the adult time and attention that the poor children of the city and region require. Thus, as this is written, "neither the nutritional nor the emotional needs of the children are being met, except through extraordinary efforts by self-sacrificing parents, and there are such parents at Arnone."[31]

Similar problems prevail at the Thomas Alva Edison Middle School in the Brighton section of Boston, a school of 650–700 pupils, grades 6–8. Edison is not a community-based school because, as this is written, most of its students are bused in from across the city. Teenage problems are exacerbated by poverty, especially the poverty of immigrant children. Most of the school's children receive free or reduced-price meals. George Cheevers teaches English as a second language to classes of fifteen and eighteen, and he also meets with even smaller remedial groups. His task is to help the children master formal spoken and written English so they can enter regular classes and be able to take the state examinations.

Cheevers continues the Brockton report. "Many of the children are latchkey children. Their parents are working multiple low-paid jobs. Many come from colonial countries with no family tradition of scholarship. Some parents are very young, some are single parents." Here the pervasive wars of consumer marketing take their toll. "Most of the kids are not involved in sports, or music, or art. They listen to rap and angry music on MTV, but they don't have the idea or the self-discipline of the social or political rebel. Instead, there is a lot of self-destructive labeling, the 'I'm-stupid' cop out. More ominously for the children's future," Cheevers notices, "the kids don't trust anyone. They have very few friends or relatives. There are really few people they can trust." [32]

Cheevers's mentor at Edison is Abe Abadi, an English teacher with a quarter century of experience. He continued Cheevers's analysis of schoolchildren's culture. "In the halls I don't hear any easy adult sorts of exchanges like, 'What did you see on television last night?' Instead they slap each other around, and if everyone is not cool, roughhousing can lead to a fight. On the other hand, they do seem open to each other. There is lots of hugging and kissing, but the question remains: How can the children learn to respect each other as human beings, not see themselves and others as objects amid all the violence, the lewd and vulgar comment? There seem to be no moral guardians for these kids. And, as always, the proud and boastful kids are the ones misbehaving. The honor medal kids are the ones who are timid and silent."

In an effective school the teachers also become a community and thereby are able to create a school culture of learning. In big, overburdened schools like Edison the teachers work in isolation, each one alone in a classroom of twenty to thirty children from seven in the morning until three in the afternoon. As Abadi put it, "Teaching is an individual act. The teacher imagines that he turns people on, as if you were a soul saver." There is much heartache in such a mission. He recalled a visit to a grocery store near his home where he saw a very bright and promising Hispanic girl, some years after she had been his student. She was now a mother, happily wheeling around three children. But, "there were so many doors she could have gone through."

"The classroom cannot combat television, radio, and commercial culture," Abadi said, without what Frank Gersony of Wakefield called a child's necessity, "strong parenting." In Abadi's and Cheevers's school they expect there will be substantial improvement only if the education community and the outside community work together to help the teachers fashion a culture of learning.[33]

Framingham, an old industrial city (population 65,000), is now a thriving western node of the Boston city region. It has bridged some of the gaps among parents, children, and teachers by reforming its system of evaluation. Starting in kindergarten, the children prepare portfolios showing what they are doing. These portfolios go back and forth from school to home so that the child, the parents, and the teachers can see the child's progress. As the children advance, the portfolio system gets more ambitious. By middle school, four times each year, each student chooses something from each course to enclose in a personal portfolio. With each enclosure, math problems, essays in English and social studies, or whatever, the student writes what he or she was trying to accomplish and what the result told about what still needed to be mastered. The portfolios are ungraded, but the teacher adds an evaluation for each submission. Also quarterly, the portfolio is sent home accompanied by a separate grade report card and general comment from the homeroom teacher.

Joan Vodoklys is chairperson for a twelve-teacher English department at Fuller Middle School (1,000 pupils) in South Framingham, the poor side of town. About 200 pupils are immigrants. Vodoklys herself teaches two English classes, one an English as a second language class for students about to be moved into the mainstream. In 1999 that class happened to be all girls, pupils from the Dominican Republic, Colombia, and Brazil. The previous January, when the schools in Brazil closed for the summer vacation, Fuller received a dozen new Brazilian students. Many of the school's girls have heavy home duties of child care, shopping, and cooking because both parents are working multiple jobs. To help these overcommitted students Vodoklys sees children for special help early in the morning before school starts, and in her office during lunchtime.

She thinks middle school is a very promising age group to work with. "Kids this age are not set; they are teachable, more flexible than high school, more willing to listen. They are very emotional and very sociable." For such pupils she tries especially to teach respect. She does this by role-playing and modeling successful exchanges before the students take over the discussions themselves. She tries to stress "their caring for each other" by demonstrating that she herself is "listening, not judging." Her goal: "If you treat students with respect, they will respect each other."

There are, of course, at Fuller "a few children who read and write poorly. There are no materials at home, and they receive no support at home. You have them for six hours," she says. "You take care of them." For Vodoklys the MCAS are a destructive innovation because she anticipates that the failing children will feel defeated and will drop out. "We may lose them unless we have more family support," she said.[34]

These teacher conversations intensify the contrast between the narrow culture wars of the schools and the active politics, institution building, and volunteering of the adults, which exists in every town and city. The groupings of communities, students, teachers, and citizens seem ill coordinated and badly out of balance.

The states of Massachusetts and New Hampshire, like states everywhere, are now mandating criterion tests for minimum levels of mastery. The results that come back clearly demonstrate the effects of poverty and class. John Conaty, an English teacher at Matignon High School, a parochial school in North Cambridge, has made a study of Scholastic Aptitude Tests. He boasts that he can guess a family's income from their children's test scores.[35] School reformers Theodore R. Sizer and Deborah Meier both stress the parallels between income and examination performance.[36] Homes without books and parents who read them, and homes that don't enjoy playing with intellectual curiosity, leave children at a disadvantage in examinations. It is not a matter of being smart or dumb. It is a question of giving a child a wealth of vocabulary, symbols, metaphors, and information that he or she can draw upon when confronted by an unfamiliar question. A poor child who studies hard and earns good grades in school still lags behind a well-to-do competitor because of this lack of stored outside information and experience. In Minneapolis in 1999, all the private school children passed the state tests, while only half the city public school children did.[37]

As has often happened throughout the history of education, those schools that address the deficits of poverty provide the most useful innovations for the improvement of all schools. Two schools located in the city of Boston, one private and one public, suggest alternatives to the current culture wars and poverty defeats.

The private school is Nativity Prep, a tiny school of about sixty-five students in grades 5–8. As its principal, Rev. Alfred J. Hicks, put it, "Nativity Prep is a Jesuit middle school dedicated to providing a quality tuition-free education to boys from low-income families living in the inner city neighborhoods."[38] Rev. Hicks advertises in the local papers and distributes leaflets in housing projects, but his sense is that most students come to him through word of mouth. He works hard to be sure that the students' families are truly poor, not just looking for a free ride. He interviews each family, saying that the children will have to work hard and will need family support and that the parents must be prepared to help out a bit with some cooking, cleaning (the boys clean the school as a regular routine, like the schoolchildren of Japan), painting, and other chores at school. Most of the households are headed by single women. The largest contingents these days are from Ethiopia and Cape Verde Islands. The school is located in a small former parochial school building that was constructed after World War II to serve the nearby veterans' children of a neighboring housing project (now called Madison Park Village). The location, off Tremont Street, next to the Ruggles T station, makes it easy to reach.

Nativity is as close to a total immersion experience as a day school can be. School classes run from eight to three, with sports from three to five. Then nearby children go home for supper and return for a seven-to-nine study hall or tutoring sessions. The more distant children are served supper by the parent volunteers. School is in session from just after Labor Day to mid-June, and then it is followed by a month of summer school–summer camp at the famous Groton preparatory school. The boys are as possession-hungry as poor children everywhere. They steal each other's food and anything that looks shiny and fashionable. But here they are taught manners and correct English. They wear neckties and leather shoes, not sneakers. There are no caps or logos or gang symbols. When you meet one of the boys, you have the experience of introducing yourself to a young gentleman in the making.

Nativity is more a family than a conventional school. Big classes have fifteen pupils, many have eight, and there is intensive tutoring. Imagine a large family whose college-age sons and daughters, nieces and nephews, volunteer to care for the youngsters. Here the staff consists of a dozen recent college graduates who volunteer to work for room and board and a little spending money for a few years. All are not skillful teachers, but they work at it, as do their charges. Inevitably there are a few "disasters," boys who fall away for what-

Chapel, Groton School, Groton

ever reason, but by the end of eighth grade the top half of the class is steaming along at a fast pace, the equal of any prep school. Indeed, Rev. Hicks finds tuition-free places in the best New England prep schools for a majority. The others are well prepared to continue in high school. Now that his school is more than ten years old, Rev. Hicks hopes that some of his graduates will return to teach.[39]

The second school is a public elementary school, now already kindergarten through sixth grade, and it will grow to include an eighth grade. It is a pilot school, one of ten such experimental schools within the budget and overall supervision of the Boston School Department. The Mission Hill School is located in Roxbury, across the tracks and up the hill from Nativity. It uses the second floor and basement of a former parochial school, Mission Hill High. The building is as cold an example of neoclassical institutional architecture as you can find anywhere. Half the pupils are African American, one-fifth Asian and Hispanic.

The school is a delight to visit. The classrooms and hallways are filled with children busy with reading, exploring, measuring, writing, calculating, singing, drawing, painting, and dancing. Altogether it is a school of 200 children learning in as many ways as imaginative children and teachers can invent. There are computers here, but the children are encouraged to explore the real world before they venture into the virtual one of screens and keyboards.[40]

Much about this school and its future have their roots in the Progressive school movement of a century ago. Thus, the Mission Hill School balances the twin themes of individual and community. The one concentration focuses on the individual learner, trying to adapt to a child's personal ways of learning, charting the uneven pathways of mastery. The other involves parents and teachers. For the parents there are frequent consultations about a child's progress, the three weekly meetings of the teachers are open to all parents, and there are potlucks and demonstrations. Parents are thought to be very much part of the school community, but they are not the ones who make the decisions about the details of curriculum, room organization, schedules, and the like. As Deborah Meier, the principal, put it, "Parents are not responsible for the results of such decisions," so they should not make them.[41] They should be consulted, however, all the time because they are ultimately responsible for the education of their children. Meier insists that in a good public school system parents would have a wide choice of different kinds of schools from which to select one appropriate to their family and children. The core community at Mission Hill is the community of teachers. This is a teacher democracy. The teachers meet three times a week. They discuss and plan the curriculum, they evaluate the students together, and they hire the new teachers.[42]

Deborah Meier is a veteran school innovator. Beginning with her first 1985 initiative, she has successfully started and run two elementary schools and one high school as small pilot schools within the New York City public school system. Despite the poverty and turmoil of East Harlem, children prospered in her schools; they were good places in which to grow up. Meier's schools, however, do not quickly or substantially alter test scores. The children learned a lot, but they did not easily overcome the competitive disadvantages of their environment. Ninety percent went on to some college education, and follow-up studies revealed that the graduates continued on to lead productive and useful lives.

Few teachers have given more worry and thought to the problem of evaluation than Meier. She now worries about what her school will do in 2001 when some of its graduating class of eighth graders fail to satisfy the MCAS. From her experience in New York and here, she advocates "patient impatience." As she puts it, "Kids have bad habits that won't change easily at home or at school. We need to be sure that they understand that we—family and school—will not give up on them, and we won't give up on the need for change either." In time of failure, "It's time for a new plan, a new deadline. If I had given up on myself the first time I tried to stop smoking I'd never have made it to the fifth time. That was the time it really worked." [43]

Deborah Meier is an extraordinary teacher who has a genius for getting excellent schools under way. Yet as a region of 1,009 public elementary schools we cannot count on a thousand more Meiers to relieve our current unhappiness with our public schools. Nor can we expect the dedicated Al Hickses to multiply to relieve our anxieties.

When you travel through the Boston region there is an inescapable contrast between the easy, informal inventiveness of town activities and the narrow confines of conflicts over public schools. Everywhere there are Little Leagues, Pop Warner teams, tennis, gymnastics, bands, dance, singing, arts and crafts, gardens, and performance groups of all kinds. Adults like working with children, but as parents we are shouting vouchers, private schools, and someone else's accountability. In the midst of this school tension, school administrators must busy themselves with testing and filling out forms while the children and their teachers long for decency and respect. The children want respect and responsibility for being citizens-in-the-making. Teachers want respect for their commitment to the children and for their hard work.

When asked about what is needed now, Deborah Meier responds, "More contact between grown-ups and kids. . . . Young people must be surrounded by grown-ups who are in the habit of exercising good judgment—who rarely have to say, 'Who, me? I'm just doing what I was told to do.' " [44] It's a definition of what it means to be a Yankee today.

Such an admonition could commence a major change in the educational politics of Boston's cities and towns. Children here, like those everywhere, have always been both a wonderful gift and a lot of heavy lifting. For all the noise they make, and for all the confusion they engender, they are not today's educational problem. Rather, it is school politics that hold back the multiplication of responsive schools.

The cities and towns of the region are sharply divided across a dozen fault lines: throwing money at education, new math, back-to-the-basics, minority rights, unqualified teachers, Godless curricula, lack of discipline, enforcing standards. These slogans of righteousness stand in awkward contrast to the more open and pluralistic life of the region's businesses and politics. They also mock our widespread and deep respect for mastery. As adults we respect skill and training in all its forms, from crafts to the new biology, from sports to virtuoso musicianship. Our numerous after-school activities show this respect in action; they are after all, small institutions of teaching and learning.

Nothing requires that the citizens of the Boston region agree on one right way to educate each other's children. Rather, we might reclaim our historic leadership in public education by fostering curiosity and education within our own adult lives, and thereby joining with teachers and children to foster a climate of learning in our public schools.

CHAPTER FOUR

Making Music

If you wish to describe the Boston region's culture as it manifests itself beyond the world of work and politics, many activities press forward to recommend themselves. The claims of the area's long and actively sustained literary tradition are strong. Yet these writers have been so much written about that it seems unnecessary to repeat that scholarship here. There are fine art schools in the region, but the visual arts have not served for the past century as a vital local tradition, as they have in Philadelphia and New York. During the 1940s and 1950s a local movement, Boston Expressionism, flourished. Although a major innovation, it received little local support and the group soon dispersed. Those interested in the visual arts can be well served by the region's many college and university museums, the Museum of Fine Arts, and the Addison Gallery at Phillips Academy, Andover.

For some reason theater is not just now flourishing in the region, but dance enjoys an ever-growing popularity. Dance groups perform everything from old-country traditional dances to classical ballet and the latest experiments. Moreover, the dancers are of every background, so that some dance companies compose a kind of snapshot of what might be called today's Boston family.

Another commentator might seek popular cultural expression in sports. Basketball, softball, golf, tennis, and football are everywhere, as they are throughout the United States. Soccer, especially, is growing in popularity with the arrival of Hispanic players. The water sports, however, give the region much of its special flavor. The sailors are triumphant. Sailboats of every size from dinghies to luxurious yachts abound. On a summer weekday morning, when the owners are off at work, you can practically walk across Marblehead Harbor on the decks of the moored boats. Every fall the "Head of the Charles" rowing meets attract hundreds of shells. In addition, there are dragon boat races, and even a club in Plymouth whose members row in open boats on the ocean. Canoeing is not the ubiquitous sport it was a century ago, but the region's rivers attract canoeists and a growing number of kayakers. Then, too, everywhere there are the nature tenders, gardeners of every level of skill and ambition, birders, sport fishermen, and hunters. In sum, the wind, the water, and the land nourish many of the favorite recreations of Bostonians.

Despite such an extensive cultural listing, many would insist that no portrait of the region's culture could be drawn without including the Red Sox and their beloved icon, the Fenway Park baseball stadium. Professional teams, however, are profit-making businesses, some even regional monopolies, so that their examination leads to yet another business story. The fans might bear watching, but being a sports fan is hardly a special cultural expression.

Consider, instead of sports, the half-million people who gather each Fourth of July on the Esplanade of the Charles River to hear the Boston Pops play a light concert that concludes with Tchaikovsky's *1812 Overture*, the cannons of the National Guard, and cascades of fireworks. The Boston Pops is a subgroup of the Boston Symphony Orchestra. And please recognize the large crowds of young people who flock to the Fleet Center sports arena and the Great Woods music park in Mansfield to hear concerts by their favorite stars. These audiences give a clue to something more deeply rooted than sports: the making of music.

On any given night, the Boston city region sends more musical

Cape Ann Marina, Gloucester

sounds toward the heavens than any other American place except
such giants as New York, Chicago, and Los Angeles. It is probably
impossible for a single author to report accurately on all this activity; surely it is impossible for someone trained only as an urban
historian. I offer my apologies in advance to the schools, groups,
musicians, and music genres that I have missed or slighted. Music
is, nonetheless, too important an aspect of modern Boston culture
to be avoided because it is so extensive that it cannot be easily sum-

marized. As Milo Miles, music editor for Soundstone, put it, "Music is an essential civilizing force because it links mind and emotions. It shapes our culture because it is something people do together. A performance is always a group process of players, dancers, singers and audience."[1]

Of course, an enormous amount of music is made by others for us to listen to. Like everywhere else in the United States we are up to our armpits in arranged, promoted, and promotional music—star turns by touring celebrities, the top 40 of every musical genre, the latest CDs, the most recent hits, the tunes of advertising commercials, and the ooze of background music. Yet, despite all this sound, there rises through the electronic flood a daily concourse of music we make ourselves.

Do we make less music now than formerly because of all the electronic sound? Surely the many family gatherings around the piano and the composition of easy household and Tin Pan Alley sheet music have much diminished. Also, professional musicians have many fewer restaurants, bars, hotels, and theaters to play in. The advent of the talking movies and the closing down of music and vaudeville in big movie theaters closed off other avenues of live music.[2] More recently, mistaken school priorities have further attacked the performance of music here. When in 1981 a state initiative mandated a ceiling on local taxes (Proposition $2^1/_2$) and forced a paring down of school budgets, administrators and parents chose to continue sports and to cut art and music training. The short-term excitement of sports took precedence over the lifetime enhancement that comes from a studying voice or mastering an instrument. Soon a quarter of the music teachers of Massachusetts were let go. Fortunately, a coalition of music teachers, educators, and musical instrument companies formed themselves into a series of organizations to work to return music to the schools. These advocates point to recent studies that show musical training helps the overall intellectual development of children.[3] Although music instruction in the public schools is now returning, a whole generation of musicians has been lost. Despite this setback, music lessons persist in many schools, as do private lessons. Moreover, the popularity of the guitar as an instrument for amateurs has vastly enlarged the ranks of players. Boston remains one of the nation's centers of music making. There are twenty-seven civic symphony orchestras in Massachusetts, more than in any other state save New York and California.[4] It is a powerful center for the repeated modern revivals of folk song and early music, it trains symphony orchestra players, and young people come here from all over the world to learn the necessary skills for careers in the ever-changing forms of popular and commercial music. The variety here is enormous, but unlike sports, there is no thorough reporting of the range of these activities. In sports the weeklies report school sports; the dailies, radio, and television handle the college and professional teams. For music, the major performers of popular music and a few local groups are covered by the weekly *Boston Phoenix*, while the dailies report the celebrities of every genre from folk to symphony orchestras. As a result, there is no place where all the various genres and interests meet each other; there is no general Boston musical conversation. The region's musical life rather more resembles the circumstances of sexual activity years ago, before it became the obsession of the public media: everyone did it, but the gossip was isolated and local.

This richness is sustained by a loose structure of musical institutions that link schools and teachers to performances, professionals to amateurs, and performers of all kinds to a variety of audiences. Because audiences here are educated and immigration-fed, the fashion limits are not strict, and the venues are many. On any given night you can hear performances that range from folk and rap to full-scale symphonies and even an occasional opera. Like much else here, the tradition of schools and colleges and the resulting intensity of education give a special quality to the music making of the Boston city region. It is the schools and the schooling that give the Boston area its unique qualities of a wide range of styles and a deep assembly of trained professionals and amateurs. These are also manifested in the many town music festivals, which range in genre from park bandstand performances through folk, quartets, and small jazz combos to large orchestras and choruses.

These local cultural processes commenced with the arrival of the first European settlers. The Pilgrims and the Puritans of the seventeenth century loved to dance and to sing, but we have no records of their secular music. Instead, they have left us books of their religious music: first, collections of English psalm tunes, then psalm tunes of local composition. Upon their arrival here the folk process commenced. Each meeting house appointed a precentor, who set the pitch and lined out the psalms for the congregation to repeat, much as we do today in a school or coffeehouse sing-along. In time the precentors drifted off the original pitch and altered the tunes. After a century of these scattered innovations, educated ministers began to complain of the low quality of congregational singing. They wanted churchgoers who could sing by the written notes.[5]

Local enterprise soon answered the ministers' calls. Itinerant singing masters, usually men of several trades, began moving from town to town, setting up month-long singing schools. They brought with them their own sheets of music for the students to copy, and two or three evenings a week young people gathered to practice singing the songs in their master's collection. At first the music was religious tunes taken from psalm collections, but by the end of the eighteenth century the masters were writing and publishing their own compositions of hymns, psalm tunes, and secular songs. Best known today of these Yankee tunesmiths is William Billings (1746–1800), a Boston tanner who wrote hundreds of songs and hymns; indeed, he was the first to make music his sole occupation.[6]

The distinguished historian Wiley Hitchcock wrote about this music and its times: "viewed historically, from a point two hundred years later, theirs was a sort of golden age of mutual participation in which teachers, composers, singers, and populace in general worked together fruitfully. If ever there was a truly popular music, the music of the New Englanders was popular . . . really the first indigenous music of the United States." [7]

Gradually this vigorous tradition was displaced by Boston's and the nation's music reformers, who raised a hierarchy of musical tastes that separated country music from city music and divided city music into layers of popular music, school music, and art music. Banished but not lost, the many editions of the tunesmiths' books carried their music south and west, where it merged with Scotch-Irish songs and African American camp meeting singing to form the amalgam out of which today's country, folk, and gospel singing sprang. Back in Boston, however, the German music of the classical era came to be established as the ruling standard of excellence.

The formation of the Handel and Haydn Society in 1815 began the process of asserting the new taste. A German musician, Gottlieb Graupner, who had played in Haydn's London orchestra, organized an amateur singing group to perform the works of the two composers. Soon a new president of the Handel and Haydn Society, Lowell Mason (1792–1872), magnified and broadcast Graupner's enthusiasm. Mason, the son of a musical Boston family, had himself been trained by a German musician in Savannah. A popular hymn collector and hymn composer, he created simple harmonies that still give pleasure, as when we sing such favorites as "Nearer My God to Thee." His importance to music in the region today rests upon his leadership of a generation of Victorians who proselytized "good music" as against popular music and the old songs of the tunesmiths.

The introduction of German music of the classical era was an enduring contribution that much enriched a provincial culture dependent on the tastes of London and its own vernacular resources. This gift, however, came at the price of separating the concert hall from the beer hall and the theater and drawing a deep line between composers of "serious" music and composers of popular music.[8] Years later, in the 1950s, the vigorous vernacular American music of the nineteenth and early twentieth centuries, the gospel songs, minstrel show dances, ragtime, and jazz, came to be reunited in the eclectic compositions and arrangement of bands, Broadway shows, and concerts. In the interval, Boston's music schools first concentrated on training music teachers and singers, then later added the training of professional instrumentalists. In so doing, they laid the foundations for the widespread music making of the region that prevails today.

Boston's first conservatory arrived in 1867 with the founding of the Boston Conservatory of Music on February 11, 1867, by the Belgian violinist Julius Eichberg (1824–93). Eichberg had succeeded Lowell Mason as director of music for the Boston schools. For many years his school specialized in string training, and it achieved some fame as the teacher of professional women string players. A successful music school that has since added opera, theater, and dance to its specialties, it has been overshadowed by its larger contemporary, the New England Conservatory of Music, founded February 18, 1867.[9]

Just as Boston's modern industrialization began with the mobilization of young farm women to tend Lowell's new mills, so Boston's most influential conservatory had its beginnings in the recruitment of young women to be music teachers and singers: school music teachers, choir instructors, singers, piano teachers, and piano tuners. Like the managers of the Boston Manufacturing Company, the New England Conservatory's founder, Eben Tourjée, stressed production. He taught students in groups so that he could cut his prices and undersell his competition. In 1853 he established his first school in Fall River, and he added three more before coming to Boston to open the New England Conservatory in 1867 (Oberlin Conservatory 1865, Cincinnati Conservatory 1867, Chicago Academy of Music 1867, Peabody, Baltimore, 1868). Tourjée offered lessons to all comers, but especially he sought to enroll young women. They in turn hoped to acquire sufficient skills to find a niche in the limited economy of the day where they could support themselves. Tourjée purchased the huge St. James Hotel in the South End of Boston (Franklin Square) and tried to keep its five hundred rooms filled with students. Like the early Lowell boarding houses, the conservatory was a sheltered home away from home, not for spinners and weavers, but for a fellowship of students serving God through music.[10]

Tourjée's administration, 1867–90, encompassed the era of flourishing amateur music making in the Victorian forms of singing and playing the piano and the organ. Home pianists played the household songs of Stephen Foster, "Beautiful Dreamer," "My Old Kentucky Home," and the like. Reams of sentimental and easy pieces were written for these keyboard players. Family and friends gathered about the piano and organ to sing secular and religious tunes; singing clubs and informal harmonizing flourished, and everywhere choirs carred on with Lowell Mason's hymns, while the more "enthusiastic" church choirs added the new urban revival hymns, like "Sweet By-and-By," to their repertoire.[11]

These too were the years of Boston's preeminence in piano and organ manufacture, the local leaders being Jonas Chickering (1798–1853) and Lowell Mason's son Henry Mason, of Mason & Hamlin, whose firm began by making parlor organs in 1859. The notable organ builders were Elias Hook (1805–81), George Hook (1807–80), Francis Hastings (1836–1916), William B. O. Simmons (1823–76), Ernest M. Skinner (1866–1916), and Charles Fiske (1925–83).[12]

Yet for all the compatibility of Tourjée's singing and piano courses with the Boston region's contemporary culture, there were never sufficient students and revenues to carry the heavy mortgage and expenses of the St. James Hotel. Fortunately, for the school and the region, the conservatory was rescued by new ambitions and new wealth. As more and more Bostonians studied overseas, especially in Germany, they brought back ambitions to raise the local standards of music and art to the levels of European capitals. One such Bostonian, Henry Lee Higginson, had studied to be a concert pianist in Vienna, but he so injured his hands that he had to stop his training. He returned to Boston and the family financial house, but in the ensuing years he established and privately funded a symphony orchestra whose mission it was to play a regular winter season of "serious concerts" and to play a series of "a lighter kind of music" in the summer. "I should always wish to eschew vulgar music," Higginson wrote, "i.e. such trash as is heard in theaters, sentimental or sensational nonsense." [13]

In 1881 the Boston Symphony Orchestra began with a German conductor and a core of imported German players. Higginson wanted his orchestra to rehearse intensively and not to disperse to freelance jobs around the city and in New York. Accordingly he instituted the rule that the players must work exclusively for the BSO, with two exceptions: they might play for the Handel and Haydn Society, and they could teach at the New England Conservatory.[14] Higginson hoped thereby that his orchestra players would not only bring the best in European music to the region but would also train a new generation of instrumentalists. His players, in fact, soon allowed the conservatory to add instrumental training to the piano and singing. In time, through such instruction, the conservatory became a nursery for the Americanization of symphony orchestra personnel in the United States.

The new wealth of the region allowed the New England Conservatory to pay off its debt and to build its present quarters next to Boston's Symphony Hall. One life-sustaining infusion of money came from a reclusive widow, Mrs. Robert Evans, wife of the president of American Rubber; a second came from conservatory trustee and music enthusiast Eben Jordan II, son of the Jordan Marsh department store founder. Mrs. Evans canceled the crippling debt; Jordan built the new building and concert hall, Jordan Hall (1903). Later he financed the building of the nearby Boston Opera House (demolished in 1958 by Northeastern University).[15]

The director who presided over this new collaboration was George Chadwick (director 1897–1930), a former conservatory student and local organist who had spent three years in Leipzig and Munich studying composition. He returned to Boston to teach at the conservatory, where his harmony book remained a standard for many years. Chadwick was not a skilled performer, but he was a very knowledgeable composer whose works were played by the Boston Symphony and ensembles elsewhere. He was an important contributor in the second wave of New England composers, among them Arthur Whiting, Horatio Parker, Amy Cheney Beach, and Daniel G. Mason.[16]

During Chadwick's tenure, the New England Conservatory became a modern conservatory. He added an opera department and started a school orchestra so that his BSO professionals could give thorough training to instrumentalists. Even with these changes, women students predominated until after World War II. As always, the women continued to meet severe prejudice. Only recently have symphony orchestras and chamber groups opened themselves to women, while in all the popular bands and combos the old prejudices persist: the women sing, the men play the instruments. Singing and solo piano, school music and home piano teaching continue to be women's specialties. For these and their male counterparts, the goal of the conservatory has been to train those students who will become teachers and amateurs to the highest level of skill possible.[17] In Chadwick's day this goal faced many obstacles. Chadwick complained that "the average student usually guesses at the time value of a group of notes or rests by the amount of ink they contain, and when they are thirty-seconds and sixty-fourths, especially if they are dotted, he loses his head altogether."[18]

Some of these pedagogical problems were solved by the establishment of a new conservatory in 1915, one modeled not on German but on French methods. The Longy School of Music is a hybrid, thoroughly American in its openness to all comers, but thoroughly French in its approach. The founder, Georges Longy (1868–1930), had come to Boston in 1898 to serve as first oboe for the Boston Symphony. While playing here he formed several orchestras and led amateurs in their music making. In 1915 his seventeen-year-old daughter Renée returned from Paris, where she had completed her training as a pianist at the Paris Conservatory. She was immediately set to work teaching eurythmics at the New England Conservatory, which had long taught solfège itself. The father, however, with his friend the BSO violinist Charles Loeffler, imagined a small school that would give American students the skills they were lacking. Solfège, a system of ear training of the Paris Conservatory, was to stand as the foundation of the new school. The singing and dictation of solfège was supplemented by Renée's teaching of Dalcroze eurythmics, a practice of steps, body movements, and gestures to encourage an emotional response to music. The goal of such training was to allow students to "hear music with both their eyes and their ears." [19]

The school continued along this path until 1925, when Georges Longy retired to France and his daughter Renée moved to the Curtis Institute in Philadelphia. Fortunately, a board member, Archibald Davison of the Harvard Music Department, took hold. His vision was to enlarge Longy so that it would include a preparatory department for children and adult beginners as well as a graduate department for performers wishing to become professionals. Under his guidance, and that of Mrs. Walter Piston, wife of the composer and Harvard music professor, the school moved to Cambridge, first to Church Street in Harvard Square and then to its present location near the Cambridge Common on Follen Street.[20]

With its enlarged program and new home, Longy, like all the educational institutions of the Boston region, became the beneficiary of Hitler's attack on Jews, intellectuals, and artists. The famous Nadia Boulanger came to teach here from 1938 through 1945, as did pianist

Lilly Dumont, violinist and chamber player Wolfe Wolfinsohn, and early music specialist Erwin Bodky. During these war and immediate postwar years, too, a kind of citywide symbiosis began to develop so that the Boston Symphony Orchestra, New England Conservatory, Longy, the Boston Conservatory, Harvard, and Boston University began to nourish one another. Sarah Caldwell and Boris Goldovsky of the New England Conservatory taught at Longy, while Erwin Bodky and E. Power Biggs, the Harvard organist, instituted an early music program, which has subsequently become a Longy specialty.[21]

Longy has continued to expand in all three of its directions: children's preparatory, adult amateurs, and professional training. With its succession of directors over the past forty years, its emphasis has veered back and forth between being a community music school and a member of the Boston professional training cluster. For the past decade, under the direction of Victor Rosenbaum, it seems to have found a stable mix that well represents much of the music-making culture of the region. Indeed, Longy's credo includes a moral purpose, a characteristic Boston emphasis since the earliest days.

The Saturday preparatory classes continue to give the best of French basic training, while Longy's adult classes mix the professional trainees with the most advanced amateurs. For the professionals, Director Rosenbaum points out, there is the advantage of a small school where the students can receive a lot of individual attention. A danger in the large conservatories is the intense competition for notice and prizes, in which, the music often gets lost in the drive to win. At Longy, Rosenbaum seeks an alternative: "We don't want to emulate this aspect of the real world. We want to teach people to foster, support, help each other. We hope that when they graduate they can go out into the world to make it a better place. Longy wants to encourage an environment of community among professionals."[22]

The establishment of the Berklee College of Music in 1945 added an important new branch to Boston's musical teaching. Berklee began as a school of jazz musicians and in time grew with the ever-changing fashions of popular music to train young people for all the branches of the American music industry—jazz, rock, songwriting, singing, jingle writing, movie music, musical electronics, and recording, as well as continuing the traditional training of music teachers for schools. This catholic expansion of Boston's music pedagogy did more than give the schools here a complete coverage of styles. It contributed to the post–World War II movement among performers to expand their repertoire, and among composers to combine the musical styles of every period and every part of the world. After the 1950s, Boston no longer followed its one-culture-at-a-time march from Germany to Russia to France but began to rove imaginatively everywhere, from the Renaissance to the present, and from the Andes to India.

Berklee's founder, Lawrence Berk (1908–95), grew up in Boston's old West End. While attending English High School he worked as a pianist in local clubs and theaters, the latter still offering live music between the films. He transcribed what he heard on records to learn something of the art of dance band arranging. After graduation from high school he tried a year of law school, but it didn't suit him. Instead, he transferred to MIT to earn a degree in architectural engineering. His graduation year of 1932 offered no jobs, so he continued his work in music. In 1934 he moved to New York City, where he found a niche for himself arranging for bands and for NBC and CBS studio music.[23]

While in New York he discovered Joseph Schillinger (1895–1943), a Russian composer and mathematician who had invented a system of composition that employed mathematical sequences and graphs. Some of Berk's fellow students were the bandleaders Glenn Miller, Benny Goodman, and Tommy Dorsey, the composer George Gershwin, and the pianist Oscar Levant. Soon Berk had mastered the system and was authorized to teach it. World War II, however, brought his engineering skills into urgent demand so he and his young wife returned to Boston, where he took a job as a design engineer at

Raytheon. He missed his music, however, and soon opened a small office on Massachusetts Avenue, near the present location of the college, where he taught a few pupils in the Schillinger method. In 1945 he purchased a house at Newbury and Gloucester streets (now Charley's Saloon) to open Schillinger House. He rented the extra rooms to instrumentalists he knew.[24]

Berk recalled that his MIT training made it possible for him to simplify the Schillinger method so that practicing musicians without much formal training could take advantage of it.[25] Most of these students in the first decade were young professionals "who wanted to be more reliable on the bandstand" or music students who transferred to find a jazz curriculum.[26] These were also the years of the bop revolution, which made the rhythms and harmonies of jazz ever more complicated. Young bop enthusiasts, like the trumpeter Herb Pomeroy, were hungry for an opportunity for organized study that would help them master the new ways. The federal G.I. Bill funded the little school's expansion so that by 1954 it had five hundred students. The training rested on jazz, and the tracks of study led to performance, arranging, or becoming a music teacher in the schools. As a signal of its success, bandleaders now called to recruit the best students, and students began to enroll from overseas.[27] In 1954 Berk changed the name of the school to its present Berklee, Berk for the father, Lee for the son, the current president of the college. In 1962 the school was converted to a not-for-profit institution, and in 1970 renamed the Berklee College of Music.[28]

The 1960s brought a revolution to this practical school of music. Folk, pop, and rock shook the school off its jazz base. As Herb Pomeroy recalled, when he started teaching at Berklee in 1956, 95 percent of the students wanted to study jazz; when he retired forty years later, 90 percent of the students were studying something other than jazz.[29] The early 1960s were the years of Joan Baez and Bob Dylan and the folk revival in Cambridge.[30] These too were the years of the Beatles, the Rolling Stones, and the British Invasion, and the gathering of an army of rock and pop performers at Wood-stock, New York, in 1969. In 1970 Boston's famous group Aerosmith was formed.

A dean later recalled the years 1966–69: "After school closed down and they gave the ensemble rooms over to the students to practice and rehearse in, that's when a lot of the new music was heard. A lot of the younger students coming directly from high school were rock players. During the day they'd learn jazz in the classroom. Then, at night, they would play what they wanted to. . . . At times it seemed like two schools were going on simultaneously." [31]

Berklee responded by building up a large guitar department and by teaching rock and funk. It also added courses for singer-songwriters who wanted to imitate the new intimate styles of Joni Mitchell and James Taylor. Jazz itself, as it passed through its phases of hot and cool, fell under the spell of electronic amplification and jazz-rock styles, while new "fusion" performers like Keith Jarrett and Chick Corea brought in the new ways of the modernist romantics. Now far from its African American dance band base of the 1930s, jazz has become a medium for individual expression by musicians who may turn to its multiple traditions or may search for examples throughout the world. [32]

Down the street, at the New England Conservatory, its new presi-dent, Gunther Schuller (president 1967–77), carried that old insti-tution along a complementary path toward personal inventiveness. He wanted his school to lead in the new experimentation and not to abandon invention to the popular performers or the university com-posers. He spoke of a "complete musician," by whom he meant a musician with a personal vision of his or her art. In 1969 he launched a full jazz program, both historical and theoretical, by raiding Berk-lee of its best performers. [33]

Today Berklee is a school of three thousand students, 40 per-cent of whom come from overseas to study the ways of American contemporary music. Of the Americans, most come directly from high school, where they were music enthusiasts and now want to go to a music school for a college degree. An extraordinary range of subjects is offered to all comers, and there is as well the traditional music teaching department, which offers a certificate that is honored in thirty-two states.[34] The college continues in its breathtaking early goal "to make an instant adjustment to a block of students or music trend" in response to the ever-changing fashions of the American music industry.[35]

The three conservatories, together with the long-established Boston Conservatory, form but one center which is surrounded by the music departments of the universities and colleges, by an outer ring of community music schools, like Indian Hill in Littleton, and by the special music programs of private academies like the Rivers School and Phillips Academy, Andover. All told, these schools offer thousands of concerts each year, and they train thousands of students to every level of proficiency. As Prof. David Hoose, symphony conductor at Boston University, put it, "Boston's music culture is both broad and deep."[36] Or, put another way, there are concerts every night, and their audiences include a strong contingent of informed amateurs. Also, although the local conservatories are not the equals of Curtis or Juilliard, the plenitude of schools means that for anyone seeking to organize a performance there is a long queue of very skilled freelance and semiprofessional musicians standing by. Finally, the openings for faculty in these conservatories, universities, and colleges attract highly skilled performers to be resident here, people who would otherwise remain in New York or Los Angeles because Boston is neither the national performance center nor a center of the American music industry.

Such an institutional configuration places the teacher-performer at the center of professional music making here, always excepting the Boston Symphony Orchestra, whose musicians have become a world unto themselves. The trumpeter Herb Pomeroy is a fine and beloved example of the local teacher-performer. Pomeroy was born in 1930 into a family of dentists. His father, uncle, and grandfather were all dentists, and the family expected him to follow that path. His mother, however, was a ragtime pianist who gave the boy encouragement when he took up the trumpet in the sixth grade under the tutelage of the local high school bandmaster. The early 1940s were a special moment for youngsters because the war had carried off so many musicians. By the time he was a junior in high school, Pomeroy was playing seven nights a week.

Then, in 1949, he went to Harvard to prepare for dentistry, but he found no place for himself in that college. Charlie Parker (1920–55), the bebop saxophonist and composer, was Pomeroy's idol at the time. He took to haunting Boston's jazz clubs to hear the new music: the Savoy and Wally's on Massachusetts Avenue, the Ken Club and Southland on Warrenton Street, and the Tic-Toc on Tremont, next to the Schubert Theater.

In the fall of 1950 he began a five-semester course of study at Schillinger House. Here he hoped to master arranging so that he might work for a big band some day. In 1952 he formed his own band. Then in the fall of 1953 he auditioned for Lionel Hampton, the jazz vibraphonist. Hampton, however, was not a good manager, and the national tour proved arduous and unpleasant. Soon Pomeroy learned that the men on the road were all running away from something—drugs, alcohol, or a bad marriage. For himself, he never drank or did drugs. Music was his passion and his escape. When the Hampton band returned to Boston's Symphony Hall, Pomeroy quit.

Now twenty-four years old and disillusioned, he thought of reapplying to Harvard, but, instead, he received a phone call from Stan Kenton to join that band in Los Angeles. From Kenton Pomeroy learned how to be a good band manager. In time, though, he tired of big band work because the fans demanded that the band pay their favorites over and over, night after night, and also because there was little opportunity for solo work. When he returned to Boston, however, he brought with him an enhanced reputation for having been a trumpeter for Hampton and Kenton. Local club owners were impressed.

There used to be a bar on Huntington Avenue in Copley Square with a basement room called the Jazz Workshop. The owner hired Herb Pomeroy's sextet to play there, six nights a week, from 1954 through 1962, when the building was condemned to make way for the Massachusetts Turnpike. A year after he began there, Lawrence Berk recruited Pomeroy to teach jazz trumpet at Berklee. This span of eight years, he recalls, was a unique opportunity for personal growth: teaching by day and playing jazz six nights a week in a small combo. Here were sustained conditions where he could try out fresh ideas and develop his own style. As Pomeroy put it, all musicians, whether jazz or classical, like best to play in small groups: "It is when we are most ourselves."

Pomeroy remained at Berklee for forty years, growing into the role of the grand old man of the jazz program. Here he taught trumpet, organized student bands and student recordings, and off and on formed his own professional band with some of his fellow faculty members. He also journeyed to Europe to participate in jazz festivals there. He recalled that when he was young and bop was the fashion, he believed that loud, high, and fast were the hallmarks of good playing. In time, however, he found his own voice; it has proved more sophisticated and inventive than the hot licks of his youth. Pomeroy is now retired from Berklee, but he continues to play about a dozen nights a month with small groups all over the Boston region. Having found in his youth a secure position as a teacher-performer, Pomeroy exemplifies the very best sort of career that Boston has to offer.[37]

Others of our professionals came here on more academic pathways than Pomeroy's training. The Borromeo String Quartet, formed in 1989, is the quartet in residence at the New England Conservatory. It is a group of young professionals who came here from the Curtis Institute of Music in Philadelphia: Nicholas Kitchen, violin; his wife,

Yessun Kim, cello; Ruggero Allifanchini, violin; and Hsin Yun Huang, viola, who replaced a founding member. Like the big bands of the 1940s and 1950s, the Borromeo is now on the road every month of the year giving concerts across the United States and Europe. Chamber music societies, city-by-city organizations of chamber music enthusiasts, make up the core of the quartet's audience everywhere they go. Kitchen says the atmosphere is "somewhat homey," perhaps a bit like the nightclub gatherings of jazz aficionados. Such an audience is a significant aspect of the Borromeo's performance these days because they are working their way through the sixteen Beethoven quartets. This music is a measure the knowledgeable hold up to judge quartets. As residents at the New England Conservatory the group also teaches students, coaches quartets, and plays many performances at schools and for charity.

Kitchen's biography tracks the steps of a virtuoso. His father, a professor of mathematics at Duke University, played piano and organ and directed the music at his church for over thirty years. His mother served as the associate concertmaster of the Greensboro (N.C.) Symphony, founded the Duke University String School, and in addition has been active in teaching music in Haiti. Nick started playing the violin when he was two, and by the time he was eight he could really play the instrument. At that moment the violinist of the Ciompi Quartet, then in residence at Duke, took him on as a pupil. At twelve Kitchen began playing concerts regularly, and later he went summers to Connecticut to attend a Yale program of the Tokyo Quartet. When he graduated from high school at sixteen he moved to Curtis, where he studied for the seven years 1983–90.

At Curtis, besides studying violin, Nicholas enrolled in conducting classes, where he found the training in music analysis very useful. The core of his experience, however, came from Szymon Goldberg, former concertmaster of the Berlin Philharmonic. Kitchen speaks of him as a wonderful teacher, "a man who demanded an intense and detailed attention to the possibilities of the music." Goldberg taught Kitchen to grapple with "the complexity that is always present in good compositions and to understand how great music only functions properly with both the depth of understanding and the most virtuosic playing." Because he expected that the level of the students' playing should rise to match what the composer had asked, Goldberg did not want Kitchen to perform too often while at Curtis. He feared that his pupil would develop bad habits from tailoring his music and his skill to the occasion. Guiltily, the young man played many concerts. Yet Kitchen carries his teacher's instruction into the rehearsals of the Borromeo. He says a group like this "can easily get a good sound which is just o.k., but it is not interesting music until it approaches the possibilities the composer has set forth." Instead, in rehearsals the group must try out and break down one system of playing after another to find an excellent one.[38]

The pianist Shizue Sano typifies the process whereby professional talent is drawn from all over the world to Boston by its schools. Sano's life journey also followed a career path of more uncertainties than Nicholas Kitchen's advance from cradle to stage, and her current situation as teacher-accompanist-performer probably well represents the situation of many Boston professional musicians.

Sano was born in Nagoya, Japan, in 1958. Neither of her parents were musicians, but she early played tunes on a toy piano. During the 1960s the piano manufacturer Yamaha opened a series of regional piano schools to encourage piano sales. Shizue started with the group lessons of Yamaha when she was four and a half, but the classes advanced so slowly that she grew bored and disruptive. The teacher expelled her from the class. Sano's father then found a composer who took piano pupils. Each Sunday the youngsters gathered to wait while he gave each a lesson in turn. Fortunately for Shizue, his waiting room boasted a generous supply of comic books.

When she was eleven this teacher intended to give her Beethoven's First Piano Concerto to work up, but he had second thoughts and instead directed her to a friend of his son's, a Juilliard-trained piano instructor. Two years later her homeroom teacher at the middle school, a woman who also served as the school's voice teacher, noticed deficiencies in Sano's technique. Thereupon she was forwarded to a new music teacher, whom Sano followed into a high school music program. While in her local high school, Sano won third prize in a national competition that enabled her to attend the prestigious Toho Gakuen School (1978–81), where Boston Symphony conductor Seiji Ozawa had studied.

In 1981 she was one of the winners of a youth competition that funded budding musicians to study overseas. The slowness of international paperwork, however, held her up for a year and a half. It was a happy accident, since it give her a chance to perform with the Nagoya Philharmonic. Finally, in August 1982 she arrived in Bloomington, Indiana, where she spent the next five years earning her artist's diploma and her master's degree. At Indiana she practiced eight to ten hours a day while studying with a number of teachers.

During these Indiana years she also entered several European competitions. Competitions can be hazardous. In 1983, while playing a Stravinsky glissando, she twisted her hand, so injuring it that she couldn't pick up a pencil the next day. Nevertheless she persevered and won a number of competitions in Belgium, France, Japan, Australia, and New York. At the Chopin competition in Warsaw in 1985 she experienced the hazards of large competitions. She had flown in from Japan, an exhausting trip. The afternoon she arrived at her hotel she was told to go to the competition hall at 2:30 in the morning to select a piano for her performance. The next few days she struggled with rotating three-hour practice sessions on pianos that were often out of tune and had keys that didn't work properly. This particular year over 140 pianists entered the competition. Sano survived the first cut that brought the group down to 40. She didn't succeed in reaching the semifinals, however, because she fell ill. "It felt like almost a miracle that I was able to get up that morning."

In June 1987 she married a fellow resident in her large coed dormitory. Together they moved to Methuen, near his job with Hewlett-Packard. Sano now depended on her conservatory network. A fellow student linked her to Roman Totenberg, professor of violin at Boston University, and a voice professor at Indiana, whose students she had accompanied, recommended her to Victor Rosenbaum at Longy. In Boston, thus, she began her career as an accompanist. Then she entered one of Menachem Pressler's annual master classes at Longy, and soon she was teaching children in the preparatory program and working as a rehearsal pianist. Today she is a regular teacher at Longy and also teaches at a private academy, the Middlesex School. This spring she is preparing for an all-Chopin recital. Given her busy schedule as teacher-performer-wife-mother she finds it hard to set aside the three to four hours each day she wants for practice.[39]

The largest gatherings of amateur musicians are the Boston choruses. Forty-odd are organized into the Greater Boston Choral Consortium, and there are probably at least two dozen more throughout the region. The groups range from small a cappella groups of sixteen singers, like the Oriana Consort, to assemblages of over one hundred, like the Back Bay Chorale and the Masterworks Chorale. Singers are generally people who sang a great deal in high school or college, and they bring every level of training to their choruses. In many groups the ages run from high school to senior citizen. Some are professionals, others read music uncertainly. Although elsewhere in the United States it is common practice to pay choral singers, here in New England only the soloists are paid. So a highly skilled chorus like David Hoose's Cantata Singers holds many professional musicians who sing for the pleasure of it. All of this activity makes a kind of regional paradox. Bostonians sing in choruses, but opera does not flourish here as it does in New York and Chicago.

Most choruses audition new candidates so they can assess the candidate's voice and test music reading skill. Those than can't sing directly from the written notes are encouraged to join nonaudition choirs where they can learn to read music. One man, Nicholas Page of Winthrop, runs his Majestic Chorus specifically as a training ground for aspiring choral singers. There are also "you-all-come" choruses, open to all, like the Belmont Open Readings, the Cambridge Community Chorus, and the Somerville Community Chorus. In these all are welcome, and in the course of time the less proficient tend to drop out and the more skilled to persist. Director David Giessow of Somerville even makes synthesizer tapes for his singers to help them learn their parts between rehearsals. In general, more women than men sing in choruses, and there is a regionwide shortage of tenors.

At Christmastime Handel's *Messiah*, a favorite with all sorts of audiences, is sung everywhere. The rest of the year programs range over the entire musical library, from early music through the standards of Bach, Haydn, and Mozart to modern composers like Gershwin, Britten, Stravinsky, Bernstein, and Pinkham. With rehearsals one night a week, choruses soon become tight-knit social groups. Indeed, college choruses are known for their high intramarriage rate. But whatever the social complexion, the great pleasure of both rehearsals and performances is what Ann Marie Lindquist, executive director of the Cantata Singers, calls "the exhilaration, the oxygen rush of joining your voice to others." [40]

Choral directors are professionals, and they follow the teacher-performer role common to the region. William E. Thomas of Phillips Academy, Andover, makes an excellent example because of the multiplicity of his musical activities. Thomas, a cellist, grew up in Lexington, Kentucky. There was much music in his family and his family's church so that his childhood piano lessons led to a lifetime commitment to music when he took up the cello in junior high school. From school he went to Oberlin Conservatory. As a junior there Thomas had become sufficiently proficient to be able to play with the Akron Symphony, a position that paid enough so that he could quit his conservatory job as a breakfast cook. Also in his junior year, an Oberlin exchange program took him to Edinburgh and Zurich to study with master cellists there. Later, for two years, he attended Pennsylvania State University on a full scholarship to earn his master's. Summers he taught strings at the Merrywood School in Lenox, Massachusetts, next to the Boston Symphony's Tanglewood. It was the mother of one of his Merrywood pupils who told him of the opening at Phillips Academy.

He joined the faculty at Phillips in 1975, a propitious time. The headmaster, Theodore Sizer, was then transforming a traditional low-voltage boys' preparatory school into a progressive coeducational school. In the process he opened up the enrollment so that Andover is now 10 percent African American and 30 percent other minorities. In such a climate Thomas found support for his initiatives.

When he arrived the student orchestra had but twenty members, and to perform it recruited adult amateurs and music teachers from the town to beef it up. Now, with Thomas's abundant energy and enthusiasm, the string players number a hundred boys and girls. During the March vacation the student orchestra makes annual tours, in the last few years to Greece and Turkey. Thomas and his string students also manage an instruction program for two elementary schools in the nearby city of Lawrence. Once a week the children who wish are bused to the academy, where Thomas gives them a short group lesson, and then twenty of his violinists give individual instruction to the youngsters.

Thomas also established a faculty quartet, the Essex Quartet, which has since changed its name to the Coleridge Quartet. The members adopted the new name to honor Samuel Coleridge-Taylor (1875–1912), a very successful black English composer who wrote in the romantic style. Thomas also directs the academy's Cantata Choir and for many years served as chairman of the school's large department of full-time and part-time music teachers.

Thomas is known in the region as a *Messiah* specialist. In 1993 Deputy Mayor Ken Reeves thought the city of Cambridge ought to have a multiracial chorus. He founded the Cambridge Community Chorus and invited Thomas to be its director for its first *Messiah* concert at the Central Square Baptist Church. Thomas has directed this open chorus of over a hundred singers ever since. The programs have included Vivaldi, Bach, Beethoven, Mendelssohn, Fauré, and Coleridge-Taylor's cantata *Hiawatha's Wedding Feast*. Each year a subgroup of the chorus sings a tribute to Martin Luther King, "A Joyful Noise," and it has been a participant in the New England Conservatory's annual Thomas A. Dorsey Gospel Jubilee. Teaching at Andover, directing the Cambridge Community Chorus, playing with the Coleridge Quartet, and doing additional *Messiah* performances, and one in Japan in 1999, keeps Thomas running. Here in the Boston region his is an essential career and role: he is one man who helped and helps hundreds to make music.[41]

Early music is also a specialty of Boston amateurs. For instance, the Boston chapter of the international Viola da Gamba Society is the most active in the nation. Early music, now defined as everything from Mozart and Haydn backward in time to the earliest surviving medieval notations, began its current wave of revival with Arnold Dolmetsch (1858–1940), a performer and instrument maker. Most of his career was based in England, but he lived in Boston from 1905 to 1911, giving concerts and building harpsichords at the Chickerings' piano factory on Tremont Street. Two of these harpsichords ultimately found their way to Harvard's music department, where they contributed to the postwar explosion of interest.

A very simplified tracking of the Boston element in the wave of early music fashion might begin with Dolmetsch and then recognize the influential performances of Wanda Landowska (1879–1959) in France and later New York, then the performances of the Scarlatti and Bach scholar Ralph Kirkpatrick at Yale (1911–84) and his contemporary the musicologist Erwin Bodky at Longy, and the recorder and singing concerts of the Trapp family of Vermont. To this sequence it would be well to add the Boston school of harpsichord manufacture, the work of former Harvard students Frank Hubbard (1920–76) and William Dowd, the work of the lutenist and publicist Joel Cohen, and the encouragement of the annual Boston Early Music Festival, begun in 1981.[42]

The significance of the revival does not rest with its return to old instruments, although these have added new sounds to contemporary performances. The important thrust of the fashion in early music is toward a new kind of music and a new relationship between composers and amateurs. Just as bebop and subsequent small combos brought fresh, clear playing into a climate of overorchestrated big band "production numbers," so the early music revival has attracted a wide public that had wearied of the incessant repetition of the nineteenth-century standards and their twentieth-century successors.[43]

There is, of course, no way to be absolutely certain how this old body of music was played. Therefore there is no right way to perform it. Interpretations range from the strictest mechanical sequence to Landowska's high romanticism. But, however it is played, the corpus of early music contains within it a substantial library of "technically simple and spiritually vigorous music."[44] A great deal of this music was written by the best composers of the times for household performance, and it is this mix of availability and quality that has drawn a large following of amateurs to recorder groups and ensembles of old instruments. These players, whose skills range from the child beginner to occasional professionals, constitute both an enthusiastic and an informed audience. They also stand as a forest of woodwinds and strings to challenge contemporary American composers who have neglected the home music makers and the ordinary Sunday choirs in their compositions.

A very skilled and attractive team of chamber players was drawn to Boston in response to an opening for early music players. Laura and Daniel Stepner had trained at Yale in the late '6os and early '7os, Laura as a violist, Dan as a violinist. After receiving her master's degree, Laura studied gamba for three years in Belgium and Europe. Dan continued on for a Ph.D., and while he was doing so he had the good fortune to study for two summers with Nadia Boulanger in Paris. When Dan was completing his studies, the opportunity opened up to form a trio at the Museum of Fine Arts in Boston. The museum was interested in sponsoring such a group because it had a large collection of antique instruments. Together with a harpsichordist friend, John Gibbons, Laura and Dan formed the Boston Museum Trio. It has been a very successful team, completing its twenty-fifth year in 1999. For many years the trio also toured Europe as members of Franz Brugën's Orchestra of the Eighteenth Century. Brugën, himself, is a celebrated recorder virtuoso.

In time the Stepners found their places in Boston as teacher-performers. Dan first taught at Longy and the New England Conservatory, and now at Harvard. In 1987 he joined the Lydian Quartet, a group in residence at Brandeis University. The quartet follows the practice of working through a body of music over several years. They are in the midst of playing modern American composers, an opportunity for Dan to exercise his interest in Charles Ives. Dan also is the concertmaster for the Handel and Haydn Society Orchestra and directs an early music festival summers in Great Barrington. Laura teaches at Wellesley College, freelances for the Emanuel Music and Cecelia orchestras, and, as Laura Jeppsen, performs with her own early music trio, Charivary. Charivary is a trio of women whose specialty is the large body of work by Marin Marais (1656–1728), the composer and musician to Louis XIV.[45]

Because most music instructors are classically trained, there are many fewer opportunities for musicians working in popular genres to find teacher-performer positions such as I have described. Beginning entrance to popular music, however, is more open to every degree of talent and preparation than is classical music, so that at any given moment there are hundreds, perhaps thousands of young Bostonians aspiring to careers in popular music.

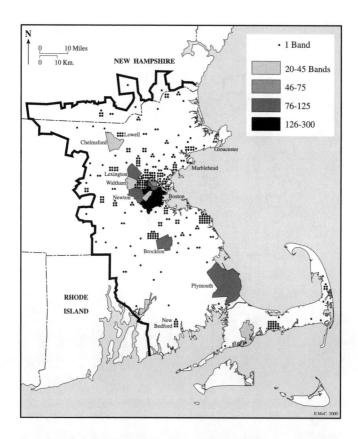

Map 9. Music Bands in the Boston Region (Band Leaders' Hometown). Source: 1997 *Boston Phoenix*

Popular music of every genre from rhythm and blues to reggae and heavy metal is a thoroughly diffused cultural phenomenon. There are bands of every stripe scatted throughout the Boston city region from Cape Cod to New Hampshire. The music makers themselves are everywhere, but the clubs where they can perform are concentrated where the young people are, in Boston, Cambridge, and Somerville, and in the clubs along the circumferential Route 95.

The hopes of a singer or a band are tantalizing, but the barriers

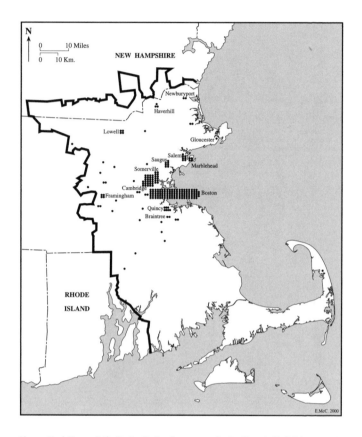

Map 10. Music Venues in the Boston Region. Source: 1997 *Boston Phoenix*. Each dot represents a music club.

are formidable. The music industry is now so arranged that the aspiring musician bears all the costs and risks. The popular music sector of the American economy is one where there is very little compensation for the many, and fabulous riches for a few stars. Scholars have described such a labor market as a winner-take-all society.[46]

All over the Boston region bands begin forming in junior high school out of the enthusiasm of kids who have had some guitar and drum lessons. They form garage and basement bands, listen to recordings, and try to imitate what they hear. If the group works well together, and if it works hard, it may win some school band contests, like the Newton High School annual playoffs. It might even advance to Berklee College's annual high school band contest.

Now comes a fork in the road. Many young people who play popular music go to Berklee to continue training in their favorite genre. Here they hope to reach a professional level of performance or to find a niche in the music business, like recording or arranging film music, or they may elect to become school teachers of music. Others stay out in the cold. They work occasional jobs at local dances and parties and may promote themselves by making a demonstration CD. Of course the band members pay for all the production costs. Local stores may take a few CDs, but the band sells most of them at its performances. The demonstration recording is also sent out to clubs in the hope of getting a gig. Perhaps a successful group that has accumulated a number of suburban gigs can use that history as a credential to break into the central Boston-Cambridge-Somerville clubs. The concentration of college and university students and young office workers in these three cities makes them a mecca for performers. The goal here would be to play the first set in rooms like Johnny D's in Davis Square, or T.T. the Bears or the Middle East in Central Square, Cambridge. On a good evening a writer from one of the city's fanzines might be there. Fanzines are small, highly opinionated throwaway newspapers, like the *Noise*, which are distributed free to clubs and record stores. Or, best of all would be an evening when a critic from the *Phoenix* or the *Globe* was there, and the band got a short favorable notice.

There are also annual moments to catch attention. Each spring a local radio station, WBCN, picks two dozen bands, often some newcomers, for a contest in which the winners receive some useful publicity. In the same season NëMO (which looks like an acronym but is a name) manages a three-day national and international conference for aspiring musicians in the popular music industry. The conference opens with an evening of local singers and bands who are given the Boston Music Awards at a rally at a big downtown theater, the Orpheum. Over the years these awards have identified a number of singers and bands that have gone on to stardom, so they are regarded as opening doors to a promising future.[47] Prizes or no, the hoped-for sequence is from local to regional to national. The first step is to develop a local following among the young people in Boston's clubs and to get some airplay from the college radio stations. A song that became a local hit would be a tremendous boost. Perhaps next, armed with some years of experience and sufficient notices, the band could book some successful regional tours, first in New England, then elsewhere. Then, somehow, by name recognition, by a chance hearing, or through a network of friends and acquaintances, an artists and repertoire (A and R) representative of one of the major recording companies might take on the group to develop a marketing package: a CD, a tour, a music video. Would it be a hit? When might stardom happen?

The gateways to regional and national recognition have, however, been severely narrowed during the past several years. The passage of the 1996 Telecommunications Act allowed the consolidation of radio and television stations. Prior to the act, local disc jockeys in each city made their own musical selections, and in doing so they often promoted local groups, like the Cars of Boston. Now, chains of stations establish programming from their central offices, and local taste is ignored. In Boston it is only the college stations and some of the public radio program time that give attention to local singers and bands.

Similarly, four giant companies market 95 percent of all CDs. Boston has but one significant CD maker, Rounder Records, and it is part of the hundreds that make up the remaining 5 percent of the national market. Television marketing has further contracted new opportunities. For some years now, popular music has been marketed nationally through music videos. It is television that sells the hits, but a band has to be well known to find a sponsor for an expensive promotion like a music video. Finally, even the booking of clubs and theaters has collapsed from a multiplicity of regional promoting companies into a national monopoly.[48] Many hope that the Internet will break the centralized control of music distribution. The hope is for direct sales of music to customers who might download what they like. Yet the Internet is so vast and its Web sites growing so rapidly that it seems likely that the same forces of advertising and promotion that led to oligopoly control of recordings will reassert themselves.[49]

At the moment, all the institutional arrangements of the popular music industry militate against innovation and local initiative. Everything is organized toward perpetuating the dominance of established singers and bands, and for the repetition and elaboration of what has been popular in the recent past. There remains, however, one powerful force for change. Despite formidable public relations and advertising budgets and careful attention to focus groups, media executives cannot predict who or what will be a hit. Audience tastes change in mysterious ways. Thus, ceaseless novelty must be offered to hold listeners, watchers, and buyers.

Despite the obstacles, a number of Boston groups and singers have persevered and succeeded in attaining national popularity. A short list might include Aerosmith, Tracy Bonham, the Mighty Mighty Bosstones, the Cars, James Taylor, Paula Cole, the Del Fuegos, Extreme, the J. Geils Band, Carly Simon, Juliana Hatfield, Morphine, New Edition, the New Kids on the Block, Donna Summer, and Throwing Muses.[50] Thus, the local singers and bands persist as long as they can hold out. Their best chance is an ever-lengthening list of club appearances. In time, perhaps a record agent or a programming executive will catch the act, listen to the CDs, and offer a national promotion.

Altogether the culture of music is a curious phenomenon. Nationally marketed music is used by young people in junior high school and later to establish their personal identity. Some learn to play their favorite music on guitars and other instruments, and a few try for a period of years to make a career in music. But whether the genre be classical or pop or folk, one constant prevails. Very, very few people can make a living as musicians.

Most professionals in the Boston region manage a lifetime of music by working two or more jobs. Paul Broadnax, a popular pianist and singer who has managed a weekend trio for years, is just such a professional. Paul came from a musical family. He grew up in Roxbury in the thirties before the postwar migrations turned Roxbury into a ghetto. His was a multiracial and multiethnic block where he was in and out of his neighbors' houses because he had to be: he started up their furnaces in the morning. As a child he was an indifferent piano student, but he took up the clarinet in high school. Although in some ways those were calmer times than now, the region did not welcome its black residents as fellow citizens. Like other black children, Paul was steered to Mechanic Arts High School and was counseled against any college courses. By the time he was a senior he had purchased a saxophone and was ready to play in local bands. He played in bands at the United Service Organizations (USO) in Roxbury until he was drafted. As an African American he was sent to the Negro platoons of the Army Air Force in Texas, where his fellow soldiers drove trucks and cleaned latrines.

After a couple of days, however, Paul was whisked off in an officer's car to be reassigned to a Special Service unit, a band. Years later he learned that the director of his Roxbury USO had arranged this transfer. Here in a twenty-one-piece band he found a mentor, a white pianist, Donn Trenner. Trenner had played with Tommy Dorsey and Les Brown, and later he would work with Charlie Parker and Stan Getz. While Paul played sax in the band, he and Trenner also played dual pianos and sang. Paul also tried his hand at learning composing and arranging. At the time he and Donn were much influenced by Nat "King" Cole, a precedent Paul has followed ever since.

When he returned to Boston, Broadnax did some arranging and playing while using his G.I. Bill tuition money to study to be an aircraft mechanic at the Wentworth Institute. Unfortunately, the moment he finished the courses the Air Force flooded the market with its veteran mechanics. Paul shifted to studying engineering in Northeastern University's night program. It has been a lifetime grievance of Broadnax that the evening program offered only an adjunct degree, not the full college credential of a bachelor's. Despite this handicap, he found a job at Raytheon from 1958 to 1973 working as a design engineer. He married and started a family in Stoughton, then the only Boston suburb he could find where a black man could safely purchase a new house.

All the while he continued performing, mostly with a trio, working weekends at weddings and suburban lounges. For many years he had a white partner, a complexion that gave the group access to gigs in the region's country clubs. Broadnax is now retired from Raytheon, and his "day job" is an Amway dealership. He is still playing piano, singing, and making CDs; the latest even includes Donn Trenner in the band. Broadnax plays at the Westin Hotel in Copley Square, in Boston's Back Bay. It is his experience that you make music because you love it, not for the money. He estimates that there is a better chance for an individual to make money in sports than in music.[51]

It is possible to mistake all the singing and playing that goes on within the Boston city region on any given night as nothing more than a loud contribution to what is going on across the nation. Yet, as a historian I hear some special qualities in our music making that seem to be nourished by the region's history and traditions.

In some of our singer-songwriters I hear a continuation of the focus on popular melodies and harmonies that characterized the former tunesmiths and hymn writers. Similarly, these singers' emphasis on their lyrics seems to connect them to the region's literary traditions as well as making them part of the contemporary wave of poetry writing and poetry readings. Some composers here, too, seem concerned to reunite the music of churches, concert halls, theaters, and nightclubs. There appears to be a strong desire to rejoin what was divided in the nineteenth and twentieth centuries by finding new musical forms, eclectic programs, and even fresh venues.

Laurie Geltman is a well-known local rock guitarist and singer-songwriter. She came here as a child when her family moved to Holliston, an I-495 fringe suburb about twenty-five miles from Boston. "Obsessed with music," she has been listening ceaselessly ever since she was four years old. She also came to poetry early, beginning by setting one poem of Edgar Allan Poe's to music. Geltman's mother supported her daughter's interest; she took her to the nearby suburban instrument store to buy a guitar and to find a teacher from the listings there. Every year from that second-grade beginning through high school Geltman took private lessons. She played every day, but not systematically. Instead, she wrote her own songs.

She purchased her first electric guitar when she was eleven. Later as a freshman in high school she joined a garage band that was successful enough to play a few suburban gigs. Through her upper-classmen friends she met a group of local musicians who took her under their wing. They gathered weekends in each other's homes for casual sessions, playing songs and jamming. Here Geltman picked up new songs, learned to play with others, and tried out solos. In the early 1980s she attended Boston University as a film major and art history minor. While at BU she teamed up with a classmate who sang beautifully. The two toured the nearby college circuit and even found some gigs on the Cape, although their possibilities were sorely constrained because they were under the drinking age. This singing and lead guitar work made her realize that her level of playing had become sufficiently advanced that she should embark on a serious music career. In her sophomore year she took advantage of the university's overseas programs to attend the American College in Paris. While there for a semester, she ran out of money, so she became a street performer outside the Pompidou Center. When she returned from Paris, she enrolled in Berklee as a film-scoring major with guitar as her principal instrument. She graduated in 1987.

Geltman regards herself as both a guitar player and a singer-songwriter. Guitar playing is her longest sustained identity, and she takes pride in her musicianship despite the conventional barriers to female instrumentalists. After Berklee she teamed up with an experimental rock band, Vasco da Gama, where she met the violinist Daniel Kellar, who has been part of her recorded work and many performances ever since.

In these postcollege years she established her own production company, Rosebloom Productions (named after her grandmother, Rose Bloom). She took on a variety of projects, often hiring a publicist to help her out. In 1992 she made her first tape, *Departure*, which attracted much local notice. Then in 1995 she recorded and released a two-song single record and sent it out nationally to college and noncommercial radio stations. One of the songs, "Paris," was used in a CD compilation, *This Is Boston . . . Not Austin, Volume Two*. Geltman and her band then made their own CD, *No Power Steering*. It was an arduous process, stretched out over two years. It moved so slowly because songs had to be recorded bit by bit as Geltman saved up sufficient funds; later she found some financial backers. After a year of aggressive New England promotion by Rosebloom the disk caught the attention of a local recording company, Eastern Front, who rereleased it for national distribution. Eastern Front's CDs are distributed by a company with a large catalogue, but it is still crowded into that marketing corner of the hundreds of companies that sell 5 percent of the recordings. As of June 1999, 230 stations played something from *No Power Steering*.

Geltman feels that at last she is getting some breaks. In the spring of 1998 she won a Boston Music Award for Outstanding

Female Vocalist. In the summer of 1999 she appeared in the Great Woods (Mansfield) Lilith Fair concerts, and she has completed a successful southern and midwestern tour. In 1999 a documentary film chronicling the lives of three Boston women musicians used "Payoff," a piece from the CD, for its title song. Her hope is to extend her audience so that her next CD will be a commercial success. All those years, however, she was not able to make a living as a professional musician. Necessity demanded day jobs: waiting on tables, catering, child care; but at last she is working full-time as a musician.

Geltman has written hundreds of songs. When she writes sometimes the tune comes first, sometimes a fragment of the words. "It is hard to get the two running together, to find just the right word." Most of her lyrics are reimaginings of experiences she has had, or knows about. Her goal is to touch the contemporary human condition with her music and lyrics. She wants to make people feel something. In her popular "Bloodline," a song about drunkenness and wife and child beating, the personal is held in tension against tradition and inheritance, "Devil's hand-me-downs rooted in the ground." Geltman explains, "I am an emotional person as an artist. I write about personal flaws. My core message is: we are all down here on the earth together."[52]

Bill Morrissey, another singer-songwriter, continues the folk tradition. In fact, he teaches that tradition to younger folk singers because he thinks that within a tradition you can find out "what works and what doesn't work, whether it's a twelve-line song or a ten-minute narrative." Like Geltman, his career has been built out of a lot of hard work, and even in these years of success he keeps pushing. "If you want to keep an audience," he says, "you must be constantly reaching out to new people." Even after seven CDs and good radio coverage by folk, college, and public radio stations, he was scheduled for 150 performances in 2000 on the national folk circuit. He plays to well-established houses, like the Arc in Ann Arbor and Passim's in Cambridge, but on Wednesdays and Thursdays, which are quiet nights, he asks his manager to book out-of-the-way places so that he can meet new audiences.

Morrissey's was a slow path to success. He was born in 1951 in Hartford, Connecticut, to an insurance family that moved around a lot. In 1965 he arrived at Acton-Boxborough High School. In the 1965–69 period, all the boys in high school tried guitars. The Beatles rode a high wave of popularity, and Thelonious Monk ruled in jazz. Morrissey learned to play guitar, to sing, and to write songs by going into the Cambridge clubs and by listening to LPs. He was not a good student, and after he graduated he tried Plymouth State College (N.H.). There he found himself totally out of place in a school dominated by fraternities and physical education majors. He took to hanging around the local music store, where he met some fellow musicians. The draft for the Vietnam War threatened, but fortunately the college neglected to inform Morrissey's draft board that he had dropped out of college.

In November 1969 Morrissey entered the life of the peripatetic folk musician. He had an acoustic guitar and a little amplification equipment, which he lugged from place to place through New Hampshire and Maine. Daytimes he wrote all kinds of songs, Dylan songs, country songs, blues, even French Symbolist songs. Most of the time he could get by on his music, but it wasn't easy. He pumped gas, worked in the mills, tried fishing in Alaska, and cleaned an Arby's while playing in Los Angeles.

A traveling singer is always a stranger in town, a nobody. One night the owner of a bar put some money in an empty beer can for Morrissey's pay. When Morrissey asked to see the bar receipts from which his share was to be taken, the owner called the police to throw him out. Another time, when playing in a bar in Haverhill, he finished his set around nine, but the boys had been drinking steadily since the mill's shift had let out, at four-thirty. A drunk came up to Morrissey to ask to play his guitar, the only one he owned. When he refused, the drunk pulled a revolver on him. The drunk was allowed to play a little. Over the years Morrissey grew smarter about one-night stands, owners, and drunks—and tougher too. He was altogether seven years on the road, playing any place that would take him. Unfortunately his start in folk performance coincided with a decline in the popularity of folk music. The antiwar and civil rights protest impetus had died down, and it took some years before audiences developed a taste for the new folk singers, like Morrissey or Ellis Paul, whose themes are the experiences of commonplace contemporary life. In the next half-dozen years, 1976–82, Morrissey found his personal voice and became one of the leaders of the new folk generation. For him, the spirit rests in the poetry of living poor in the mill towns of New England.

Ironically, the gentrification of Portsmouth, New Hampshire, nurtured Morrissey's advance. This city, an old seaport and mill town just across the border from Massachusetts, began in the late 1970s to enjoy a boom in restored homes for commuters and summer people. With the restorations came tourists; restaurants and clubs multiplied, and here Morrissey found steady work. He took up residence in nearby Newmarket, where he lived with the daughter of a professor of creative writing, a novelist, Thomas Williams. Williams taught Morrissey the ways of simplicity in writing.

Then after twelve years of apprenticeship in the far hinterlands of Boston, Morrissey moved to Cambridge in 1982. He soon received a favorable notice in the *Globe* for his opener at a Tom Paxton concert. A woman friend who sang at a Greenwich Village club, Kenny's Castaways, often sang one of Morrissey's songs. It was the proprietor's favorite, and he gave Morrissey a once-a-month gig. Another favorable notice appeared, this time in the *Village Voice*. Later he was invited to play at a big Christmas folk show at Boston's Symphony Hall. There the organizer of the Newport Folk Festival heard him and invited him to perform the next summer. Now he was on his way, seventeen years after he had dropped out of college and taken to the road as a folk singer.

When he started singing Morrissey noticed that those around him were singing of prairies, farms, even railroads, places they had never been, times they had never known. Instead of adopting these conventions, he cultivated his penetrating eye for the life around himself. Thoreau could see in the scampering of the squirrels the planting of the next oak forest. Morrissey can see the spirit of life in the confinement and weariness of the working poor. In 1996 he published a short novel, *Edson*, about a dying mill town, and he is now writing another novel in the time between gigs.[53] My favorite Morrissey song is "Different Currency," a song of a waitress.

> **He wasn't much to look at**
> **but she didn't really care.**
> **She was pretty sure**
> **his car was good enough to get her all the way down there.**[54]

Daniel Pinkham is the leader of Boston composers who have tried, or who are trying, to bridge professional and amateur music making in their compositions. He is also unique in his attention to the Sunday choir. The great-grandson of Lydia E. Pinkham, the purveyor of patent medicine, he was born in Lynn in 1923. His parents were not particularly musical. His grandmother had attended the New England Conservatory when it had a branch in Providence, and she played the piano. His father continued an interest in the banjo from his undergraduate days at Brown. Like many children, Pinkham began piano lessons when he was five. His musical training started in earnest, however, when he was fifteen and entered Phillips Academy, Andover. There he studied with Carl Pfatteicher and took all the harmony and music courses the academy offered. For that era Wagner was the preeminent composer; Wagner was "real music." But, for Pinkham the defining moment came when the Trapp family (now famous from the film *Sound of Music*) of Vermont stopped on its first tour (1938) at the academy. The Trapps had a tiny harpsichord, a viola da gamba, and a quartet of recorders. They were eight singers in all. "When I heard this fresh, simple, clear music, it turned me on."

The next year Pinkham bought a little German-made clavichord and began his lifetime interest in early music. He studied harpsichord at Harvard and played the Dolmetsch Chickering there. Later he studied with Wanda Landowska and took organ instruction from E. Power Biggs. In time he became the harpsichordist for the Boston Symphony Orchestra. At Harvard in the 1940s he also had the good fortune to study with Nadia Boulanger, Walter Piston, and Aaron Copland. He never regarded himself as a singer, but he sang in Boulanger's ensemble. "I could find the pitch, and I could count," he recalled.

His career as a teacher-performer-composer blossomed at the Boston Symphony's summer Tanglewood program, where he worked with the choruses. There he wrote songs and circulated them in manuscript. The San Francisco music critic Alfred Frankenstein wrote enthusiastically about these vocal compositions. Soon commissions for compositions began to come to him. In this work, both the clarity of early music and Stravinsky's neoclassical emphasis on small instrumental combinations showed their influence. Over the years this work has embraced four symphonies, piano and organ concertos, chamber music, electronic music, and scores for twenty television documentaries. The commissions are still coming in. He has taught at Simmons College, Boston University, Harvard University, and since 1957 at the New England Conservatory.

Pinkham's role as a performing musician has made him attentive to the availability of his compositions. To his youthful enthusiasm for the clarity of early music he has added the experience of Kapellmeister. In 1958 he became the organist and choirmaster for King's Chapel, the nation's oldest Unitarian church. This position has encouraged Pinkham to explore oratorios, cantatas, and organ music, and it has directed his attention to the role of amateurs. He enjoys working with amateur choruses. As he says, "It is a social activity; you get a lot of feedback." To his mind there has been in recent years a "dumbing down" of church music: too many primitive do-it-yourself guitar masses and pop songs that do not help the parishioners with their piety. For Pinkham, inexperienced choirs deserve and thrive on well-conceived, simple contemporary music. Like his nineteenth-century predecessors, he wants to use church music for moral purposes: "Handel used to say that he hoped not only to entertain people but also to make them better." [55] Both in his church and in his secular music Pinkham tries to write music that amateurs can sing and play. "Of course when the Boston Symphony plays my music it sounds great, but what I write does not require a BSO skill level to be performed and enjoyed." Live music performances, not recordings, are Pinkham's pleasure.[56]

Pinkham has had the good fortune to be the beneficiary of the Boston Symphony's tradition, set by Serge Koussevitzky (conductor, 1924–49), when the orchestra happily joined two functions both by serving the local creative community and by becoming one of the leading orchestras of the nation. It continues as a national treasure, and it still gives many concerts for public school children. Indeed, it has enlarged its educational work in new ways. Yet, somehow, this outreach has yet to capture young audiences for Symphony Hall. For his part, Pinkham has had some success in popularizing the support base for public concerts. When he came to King's Chapel in 1958, the parish catered to a small circle of old Boston families. It was not the city institution it has since become. Pinkham proposed a series of public concerts. The board calculated the expected loss and said they could raise the money among themselves. Instead, Pinkham instituted a universal sponsorship. The concerts are now guaranteed through a wide mailing to subscribers.

Such a useful social innovation links Pinkham to younger composers like Scott Wheeler of Dinosaur Annex and others who are seeking new settings for the performance of contemporary music. In

Wheeler's professional lifetime the "serious music" community of Boston, like those elsewhere in the United States, has been torn between extreme poles: the twelve-tone followers of Arnold Schoenberg such as Milton Babbitt, Irving Fine, and Arthur Berger versus the experimentalists such as John Cage, Morton Feldman, and Christian Wolff. A middle group, the eclectics, has also developed between the two camps, people who have merged jazz, twelve tones, and the methods of older classical composition. These are composers such as William Bolcom and MIT's John Harbison and Peter Child. The eclectics are often called "neoromantics," even though their compositions are not romantic at all. The label is assigned because they use cantabile lines of melody, which have an immediate appeal. In recent years the conflicts have been bitter because they have taken the form of struggles to control university music departments.

There seems, to an outsider, to have been an abatement of the isolation of the separate groups in recent years, and now it is possible to entertain hopes for new opportunities for connections among composers of the various schools, professional performers, and amateurs. Here the catholicity of the New England Conservatory sets the example. As Scott Wheeler put it, "The New England Conservatory is a wonderful place. It is open to every style of music from experimental to extreme academic. It is a delightful place, but it lacks sufficient money to hold on to the most successful composers." The universities lure them away by offering high salaries. Thus, for Wheeler, Harvard, MIT, and Brandeis dominate the local world of music composition. Wheeler's own position, however, suggests that there are alternatives to academic performances of new music.

Wheeler was trained at Amherst College and Brandeis University, and he worked under Virgil Thomson. For a number of years he played jazz in the clubs. Now for the past twenty years he has taught music in the theater program at Emerson College. Thus, he stands a bit to one side of both the conservatory and the Ivy League universities. He thinks his angle of vision suggests to composers fresh possibilities that could be learned from clubs and the theater. Wheeler has written a great deal of piano and chamber music, but he also has written large choral pieces and theater music. He is working on an opera and has been commissioned to write songs.

A good deal of Wheeler's performance time is taken up with the Dinosaur Annex, where he conducts and plays the piano. Dinosaur Annex began as a composers' group like Collage and Composers with Red Sneakers. It was formed out of a dance company in 1975–76, the "Annex" in its name stemming from the dancers having been annexed to a theater group. Rodney Lister of the New England Conservatory took the lead, and Wheeler from Emerson and Ezra Sims, a microtonalist, completed the founding trio. The initial concept was to offer programs that mixed works of contemporary composers with classics. The classics, in turn, were to be chosen to break down established hierarchies. Thus, Cage and Percy Grainger appeared on the programs together with the founders' compositions.

In 1982 the Dinosaur outlook shifted to a concentration on music composed during the last ten years. Concerts are given in the First and Second Church in Boston's Back Bay, and at Sanders Theater at Harvard. The group also tours. Some feel the Dinosaurs have drifted too far from the experimentalists and that their offerings are now "neoromantic." Wheeler's goal as a conductor and organizer is to offer new compositions in ways that are as far as possible from academic settings. He wants new music to be thought of by the public the way people think of theater and jazz: as an evening's entertainment. He hopes to find a venue where the Dinosaurs might play while wine and beer were served to the audience. Some years ago the Composers in Red Sneakers introduced humor and fun into their performances. Wheeler thinks the next step is for composers to have their music performed in the same sort of settings as the best jazz clubs, like the Regatta Bar in Cambridge and Scullers in Boston.[57] For the composers this also means not seeking the most personal and esoteric of musical language. As Dan Stepner put it when describing the work of the Lydian Quartet in choosing music for its current series on American composers, "A successful piece of music should have sufficient available material so that an audience can comprehend and enjoy it at a single hearing." Or, put another way, in a region full of conservatories, colleges, universities, and music schools Boston doesn't need more concerts. Instead, perhaps it needs more ways for its composers, professional performers, and amateurs to make music together.

In sum, the musical culture of the Boston city region runs along the common courses of American music, but it also has its unique emphases and qualities. It is surely a nursery of folk and early music genres, a seedbed of choruses, an exemplar for classical music, and a training ground of highly skilled professionals in every genre. For both newcomers to the region and residents it is a rich gathering of music-making communities. To those, like myself, who try to encompass all this activity in one overview, we take heart in a little story that the composer Charles Ives (1874–1954) told about his father, the town bandmaster. "Once a nice young man (his musical sense having been limited by three years of intensive study at the Boston Conservatory) said to Father, 'How can you stand to hear old John Bell (the best stonemason in town) sing? Why he sings off the key, the wrong notes and everything—and that horrible raucous voice— and he bellows out and hits notes no one else does—it's awful.' Father said, 'Don't pay too much attention to the sounds—for if you do, you may miss the music.'"[58] I have tried here to listen to the music my fellow Bostonians make.

CHAPTER FIVE

Changing Places

The city region of Boston has not grown rapidly during the post–World War II years. Since 1950 its four-decade population increase was 32 percent, but half the national average. Massachusetts and New Hampshire are not Californias. They grew up when the nation was young so that during the twentieth century, like some attractive middle-aged couple, not growth but change describes their recent experience. For the immediate future, the best guesses imagine that the current regional population of 4.7 million will continue its modest pace.[1]

Yet modesty makes its demands, and a 32 percent increase in regional population required places to live for an added 1,133,000 inhabitants who hadn't lived in Boston in 1950. Not only did these newcomers demand new facilities, but new and old residents together took up new ways of living, thereby making some places desirable and others unwanted. The city of Boston lost 260,000 inhabitants, while southern New Hampshire and Cape Cod each gained 140,000. Derry, New Hampshire, boomed from 6,000 to 30,000, Tewksbury, Massachusetts, from 8,000 to 27,000, Holliston from 4,000 to 13,000, Franklin from 8,000 to 22,000, and Plymouth from 14,000 to 46,000. Overall, these four decades of population growth and new ways of living meant that in the old core cities and suburbs within the circle of State Route 128 there was a small net loss

	Population		Change	
	1950	**1990**	**Number**	**Percentage**
Boston City Region	3,564,000	4,697,000	1,133,000	32
Inside Route 128	1,933,000	1,764,000	(169,000)	−9
Beyond Route 128	1,631,000	2,933,000	1,302,000	80
Cape Cod	47,000	187,000	140,000	298
New Hampshire	62,000	202,000	140,000	226

of 9 percent. Here the heavy losses of the city of Boston and some old industrial satellites were partially offset by small gains in neighboring cities and towns. In the vastly larger area from Route 128 to the edges of the Boston region, growth was rapid and substantial, 80 percent (table 3).

As a consequence, the social geography of Boston now resembles that of other American metropolises where the centers have at last stabilized and the edges continue to catch the dispersing metropolitan population, places like Chicago, Minneapolis, San Francisco, Portland, and Seattle. Estimates for the future guess that the old core of Boston, Brookline, Cambridge, and Somerville will prosper anew with the finance-service-science economy, while the neighboring suburbs will show small gains or losses as they have since 1950. Change in these suburbs has been driven by the reduction in family and household size, not by out-migration. Thus, Belmont, Watertown, Medford, and Malden have lost population but not popularity. The outer areas beyond the 128 semicircle will therefore have to continue to accommodate most of the region's growth.[2]

Social, cultural, and economic events have driven these changes, but the new patterns rested upon a transportation framework that was constructed during a decade and a half from 1950 through 1965. Since that time, the transportation projects undertaken have consisted of incremental improvements to the 1965 frame. For example, the multi-billion-dollar "Big Dig" merely upgrades the old Central Artery that runs through downtown Boston, while the new extensions of commuter rail service beyond Route 128 merely reestablish lines abandoned during the 1950s.

The highway building boom of 1950–65 served as the facilitator for the new social, cultural, and economic ways of Greater Boston. It did so by establishing a giant regional highway grid formed by the interlacing of limited access highways with the older state and federal routes in the area from State Route 128 to I-495 and beyond. Here the two circumferential freeways tie together the outreaching radials to form a complete multidirectional system. If a driver be patient enough to endure traffic jams on the freeways and intersection waits on the old roads, it is possible to go with some expedition from any one point in the outer Boston region to any other. Once completed, the new highway frame reinforced the region's class

Downtown Boston from Piers Park, East Boston

and racial segregation, and it facilitated a semirural lifestyle that is popular with so many Boston households. It also brought cheap, accessible land to industrial and commercial developers.

Such far-reaching effects cannot be said to be the intentions of the highway planners and builders of the boom era. Theirs was the limited focus of traffic counts. By so restricting themselves, they narrowed the Boston region's tradition of parkway and park planning to the vestigial remnant of roadside grass. As a consequence, their giant grid stands without any organized principle of either land management or urban development.

In 1948 the state legislature finally responded to a widespread pent-up demand for relief from stop-and-go traffic and the clogging of Main Streets everywhere. Before the new highways, it could take an hour to travel from Belmont Center to State Street in Boston, or to cross the Charles River from MIT in Cambridge to Wentworth Institute on Huntington Avenue in Boston's Fenway. Such modest improvements as the sequentially timed traffic lights of Commonwealth Avenue in the Back Bay made these few blocks seem like an expressway. In 1948 a constitutional amendment passed requiring that all the proceeds of the state's gasoline tax be devoted to road building (Article 78). That same year, after a prior Republican refusal, a new Democratic legislature authorized a huge bond issue for highway construction. Thus it was that the proposals of the planning report of that year, *The Master Highway Plan for the Boston Metropolitan Area*, came to be realized. To appreciate what is new and what is old in the freeway framework it is necessary to realize that most of the new work merely enlarged the historic pathways of the Boston region. The new highways continued the old pattern of the center city next to the harbor with roads and rail lines radiating outward.[3]

The freeway building era opened with the Mystic River Bridge in 1950. It closed with the linking of the Massachusetts Turnpike (I-90) to the downtown Central Artery in 1965. The Mystic River Bridge and

Tobin Bridge and New Houses, Charlestown

the later Callahan Tunnel (1961) repeated the paths of the former East Boston ferry and the East Boston Streetcar Tunnel (1904, now called the Blue Line Tunnel) and the Sumner Tunnel (1934). The Central Artery through the downtown (1959) followed the path of the nineteenth-century Atlantic Avenue wagon and rail improvement for the wharves; the Massachusetts Turnpike (1957) re-etched the lines of the Worcester Turnpike and the Boston and Albany Railroad; the Southwest Expressway (I-95, south) repeated the Providence Turnpike and the main line of the New York, New Haven and Hartford Railroad, but citizen opposition stopped its linkage within the city of Boston. The Southeast Expressway (1959) followed the old Dorchester Avenue Turnpike and the Old Colony Railroad. Its connection to an improved U.S. Route 3 formed a superhighway to Cape Cod. I-93 north to New Hampshire opened in 1964, and with the improved north section of U.S. 3 and State Route 2 the group repeated the old Middlesex Canal and the main routes of the Boston and Maine Railroad to Lowell and Fitchburg.[4]

The highway building boom halted when popular consciousness shifted. The public came to enjoy the relief of traffic jams on Main Streets and in downtowns, but they also began to experience the sudden and massive traffic jams that freeways exhibit. Some of the public also learned that the new highways did not make good neighbors: their rights of way required massive land seizures and home destruction, and those who lived next to the roads suffered the ceaseless highway roar. In 1970 a citizen outcry against urban highway building, led by opponent Jim Morey and later endorsed by Boston's mayor Kevin White, united citizens in Cambridge and Roxbury to force the then-governor, Francis Sargent, to declare a moratorium on all highway construction within the confines of the Route 128 arc.[5] Later the governor spearheaded a successful campaign for new federal legislation to allow the use of federal highway funds for public transit improvements. Subsequently, the state has extended its transit lines (Red Line to Braintree, 1980; to Alewife, 1985; Orange

First Church in Roxbury (1804), Eliot Square

Line reconstructed, 1987) and it has rebuilt and extended former commuter rail lines. In the outer area, highway building extended the grid to southeastern Massachusetts. The former rail links to Fall River and New Bedford found freeway expression in a new Massachusetts Route 24, and its New Bedford connector, Massachusetts Route 140. Finally, a freeway link from Wareham to Providence along the shore of Buzzards Bay repeated U.S. Highway 6, and the New Haven Railroad line to the Cape.[6] Also, the freeway transformation of Route 44 from Plymouth to Providence is commencing.

The two circumferential roads, Routes 128 and I-495, which form the crosshatching of the region's highway grid, were born of a somewhat different history than the radial repetitions of 1950–65. They are, instead, the lean and pinched offspring of a half-century of park and parkway planning.

In 1875, after two favorable referendums, the city of Boston began to plan and build what became, after twenty years of construction, networks of parks and parkways. The longest series ran from Charlesgate in the Back Bay through the Fens and along the Muddy River to Jamaica Pond, the Arnold Arboretum, and the huge Franklin Park. A parkway wound through these parks so that horseback riders, people in carriages, and bicyclists might enjoy the scenery. The parkway itself, roads like the Jamaicaway and the Arborway, took the form of a continuous planting of trees and lawn on the side of the road. To preserve this green edge curb cuts were restrained, often by the addition of a parallel service road. Unlike a freeway, however, full intersections crossed the parkway wherever it met important city streets.[7] The parkway's margin later reappeared as the very model of the mowed grass that borders the freeway. Such indeed, was the road design promised by highway planners in 1948 when they set forth the definitive proposals for Boston's freeway spider web.[8]

The designer of the Boston Park system, Frederick Law Olmsted, intended to extend his parkways down what is now Columbia Road

Edwin Street, Dorchester

to make a circuit to the beaches of Dorchester Bay. It remained for his young associates, Charles Eliot (1859–97) and Arthur A. Shurtleff (1870–1957), to carry such thinking on to metropolitan fruition. The creation, in 1893, of the Metropolitan Park Commission, following on the precedent of the Metropolitan Sewerage Board (1889), gave the young men the institutional base they required to propose and construct a ring of coordinated parks and parkways. (The separate boards were consolidated into the Metropolitan District Commission in 1919.)

Eliot built his metropolitan goals upon the Boston precedents: the design of parkways should enhance the natural beauty of the existing land form; open space should be preserved at the fringe of dense settlement so that the general public might find access to walk and play; public reservations should be open to all Massachusetts residents and be easily reached by public transportation; and land should be acquired in advance of settlement so that as the urban region expanded it would grow with an adequate supply of open space for pleasure and recreation.

To reach such goals Eliot proposed that the Metropolitan Park

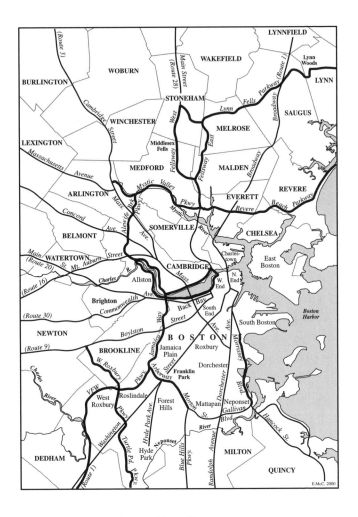

Map 11. Post–World War I Parkways and Thoroughfares

Commission begin a fresh series of projects: beaches at Revere and Nantasket to supplement the existing South Boston facilities; embankments, parks, and parkways for the Neponset, Charles, and Mystic Rivers, and four new giant wilderness parks at the Blue Hills, Hobbs Brook, Middlesex Fells, and Lynn Woods. These four new parks lay at the termini of street railways eight to ten miles from the center of Boston. Only the Hobbs Brook was not constructed because the city of Cambridge seized much of the proposed parkland for its reservoirs.[9]

After World War I Bostonians rushed to purchase cars, and this automobile infusion fostered a steady advance of suburban settlement into the towns now encompassed by the metropolitan park system. West Roxbury, Newton, Belmont, Arlington, Medford, and Lynnfield sprouted single and two-family frame houses. A transit study of 1945 reported the effects. The three commuter railroads of Boston in 1920 served seventy-nine million passengers, but by 1941 the passenger count had declined to thirty-four million. Within the same period the core cities of Boston, Cambridge, Chelsea, Everett, Malden, Revere, and Somerville commenced what would later become decades of population decline.[10]

The post–World War I automobile diffusion called forth two responses: the building and planning of circumferential roads and the proposal for an outer greenbelt of parks and parkways.

In the hope of relieving traffic jams at the center, the Metropolitan District Commission built the region's first circumferential highway during the late twenties and early thirties. The new road was a four-lane parkway that began in Lynn on the north and then ran through the Lynn Woods to the Middlesex Fells, to Medford, and then along the Mystic River across Somerville and Cambridge to the Charles River, thence down the Charles on its north bank, Memorial Drive, until it crossed the river on the new Cottage Farm Bridge (now called the Boston University Bridge) to join the existing Boston parkways in the Fenway that carried cars to Jamaica Pond and Neponset.[11] It was this winding series of parkways that later served as the precedent for the controversial inner-belt interstate highway loop.

The future Massachusetts Route 128 circumferential freeway also found its beginnings in these years. It first emerged in 1925 as part of a numbering project. In that year the federal government numbered its routes—U.S. 1, U.S. 20, and so forth. Accordingly, an official in the Massachusetts Department of Public Works did the same for the roads of state responsibility. He labeled a series of town roads and streets to make a circumferential route with 128 as its number. On the south it began in Hingham and then made its way through a ring of towns from Milton to Dedham, Needham, Waltham, Lexington, Woburn, and Wakefield, to end on the north in Salem.[12] About this time, too, the Metropolitan District Commission seems to have been prodding the state Department of Public Works to add a ten-mile radius route to the MDC parkway circuit then under construction.[13]

Planning for such a road definitely had commenced at this time under the direction of Franklin Calhoun Pillsbury (1869–1937), a project engineer for the Department of Public Works. Pillsbury had come to Boston from Chicago to work as an artist, but he subsequently took up the practice of civil engineering, first in a private firm and then for the commonwealth. In 1923 the department appointed him project engineer to take charge of all surveys, designs, and cost estimates for new roads. During his tenure (1895–1937) he laid out all the major routes of eastern Massachusetts.[14] In 1928 the state Planning Board and the Department of Public Works recommended to the legislature that Pillsbury's "Great Northern Circumferential" be constructed. Subsequently, between 1936 and 1941 eight and one-half miles of double-barreled highway between Peabody, Danvers, and Lynnfield was completed. The resulting road was a plain, unornamented knock-down version of the then style-setting Merritt Parkway in Connecticut.[15]

The interwar automobile dispersion of Boston also called forth proposals to continue the tradition of park and parkway planning and land acquisition, but this time fifteen to twenty miles out from Boston's State House. A governor's committee recommended that a ring of green spaces be built along a new circumferential parkway. The new greenway, called the Bay Circuit, like its predecessors, was to begin and end at the Atlantic shore beaches, on the south at Duxbury, on the north at Plum Island in Ipswich, Rowley, and Newbury. It was to pass through Sharon, Foxboro, Sherborn, Concord, Andover, and Wenham. The plan envisioned joining up some existing parks and forest reservations as well as acquiring new ones to make a continuous greenway.

Had the parkland been purchased and the parkway been built, it is fair to imagine it as resembling the Rock Creek Park and parkway in Washington, D.C. One of the leading advocates of the Bay Circuit, Charles Eliot II, was fresh from that Washington project.[16] The Trustees of the Public Reservations and the Appalachian Trail planner Benton MacKaye tried to keep the idea alive, but the Great Depression and World War II put an end to the realization of such ambitious schemes. Perhaps support failed because at a time of economic failure few politicians or voters could imagine a metropolitan wave of building that would fill the fifteen- to twenty-mile area with new houses and businesses.[17] In recent years the Bay Circuit Alliance has formed with the Trustees of the Public Reservations, the National Park Service, and volunteers to preserve existing greenways along the Bay Circuit corridor and to encourage towns to establish trails and bikeways.[18]

The greenbelt idea is an attractive one, especially so to a generation like ours that is overrun by patchwork development. Nevertheless, it is well to realize the special orientation of the 1920s proposals. Charles Eliot II and his Trustees supporters were park planners who imagined families from a densely settled city venturing out to country parks for strolls, picnics, and canoeing. Today automobiles carry the residents of the Boston city region easily 100 to 150 miles to country places and ocean shores where roadsides and parks have been reformulated to accommodate automobile visitors. In the new patterns of recreation, some of the old wilderness parks, like the Blue Hills and Middlesex Fells, are underutilized because they have not yet been readapted to contemporary tastes. Moreover, the former park and parkway planners did not focus on the maintenance of healthy urban ecosystems, as we must now. The old parks did not cohere to conserve wildlife corridors and reserves or protect water resources. They saw green as a relief from a dense city landscape of houses, factories, and stores. We now live at much lower densities; in fact, most Bostonians live in an urban forest, and we travel about with an average of 1.1 persons per automobile.

The completion of the eastern Massachusetts highway grid by the construction of its two circumferential highways was by no means the sole cause of our current urban circumstances, but it did transform the area outside Route 128 into one vast land market. It also divided the Boston region into two transportation zones: the zone inside Route 128, which can often be negotiated with public transportation, and the zone beyond Route 128, where residents must have access to private automobiles.[19]

Immediately after World War II ended, construction of Route 128 began again. By 1957 a four-lane divided highway stretched in a half circle from Lynnfield to Braintree, but traffic already exceeded its capacity. Fifty bridges were then torn down and rebuilt to accommodate an enlarged six-lane road that reached completion in 1963. To accommodate the wishes of federal highway planners who sought to define a continuous Maine to Florida highway, a large segment of Route 128 was renumbered to be I-95.[20]

As the 128 reconstruction went forward, federal highway planners encouraged cities like Boston to construct a succession of ring roads so that traffic might travel easily across the radial highways of hub-and-spoke metropolitan regions. What became I-495 followed this regional design. Like its earlier companion, which first appeared as a new bridge in Lynnfield, I-495 appeared in 1961 at Westford, outside Lowell, in the modest guise of a "relocation of Mass. Route 110." (Route 110 also wandered through farms and towns much as old 128 had, only in this case the path ran from Worcester to Lawrence.) By 1970 an ample six-lane freeway stretched from Amesbury and I-95 on the north, along the edges of the cities of Haverhill, Lawrence,

Lowell, Marlborough, and Milford to a southern junction with I-95 at Mansfield. By 1983 the arc had been extended to a southern terminus at Wareham and I-195.[21]

The contemporary Boston city region that the freeways helped to establish is by no means a simple place of cities and suburbs. The new expanded region, especially the vast developing tracts beyond Route 128, is far more various than the old core cities and their suburbs. The new region surpasses the old in heterogeneity because it draws upon so many different histories, so many different peoples, and so many alternative adjustments to the disciplines and possibilities of contemporary America.

Such variety overwhelms any short description, but a sense of its range can be gauged by examining some of its alternative manifestations: Ipswich, a postcard New England town; Lawrence, a city some call the nation's first industrial park; Framingham and Natick, old towns within a busy cluster that thrive on the new economy; and the "2020" effort, in which town and business leaders are trying to organize the fifty-one cities and towns of the booming Massachusetts Lakes District for growth management. In each case the meaning of the variations can be estimated by noting something of the history of the town or area, something of the condition of the land, and something of its residents, and by examining its relationship to the larger Boston city region.

I P S W I C H

Ipswich is an early settled seventeenth-century town (1634) that today resembles everyone's image of what a New England town ought to look like. Although only twenty-five miles from Boston, lack of highway access has preserved it. The old U.S. 1, which enlarged the turnpike from Chelsea to Newburyport, lies at a far corner of the town, and Route 128 and its connecting freeways stand some miles away. The Metropolitan Bay Transit Authority has continued its rail service with thirteen trains to Boston each weekday, but rail commuting has not, as yet, engendered a land rush. Industrial progress and suburban advance have both touched lightly on the town whose best-known industry is the digging of clams.

The narrow village streets are lined with an agreeable mix of three centuries of wooden houses. There are white churches, high-ceilinged stores with apartments above, and the largest collection of still-standing buildings erected in 1725 and earlier that exists anywhere in the United States. Main Street even crosses the Ipswich River on a stone arch bridge constructed in 1764.

The village is but one of Ipswich's postcard scenes. The softly rolling fields of local farms line many of its main roads, while the Atlantic ocean edge offers spectacular white sand beaches, a barrier island reservation, and a perfectly beautiful expanse of tidal marsh. This Great Marsh has long been a favorite subject of landscape painters. Thus, Ipswich village, farms, and oceanside compose a pastoral landscape that tourists flock to, and Bostonians visit with pleasure.

Of course, like all the region's towns, it has a mill next to the river. Industrial Ipswich began with stocking knitting. In 1822 two English Nottingham stockingers brought their hand-powered machines to town. Here the trade was carried on in small backyard shops, much as shoes were made before the giant steam-powered factories. The men ran the knitters to make cotton or woolen tubes, and the women sewed up the toes. In 1868, Amos Adams Lawrence (1814–86), a member of the leading textile family, built the present mill near the dam to make stockings with power machinery. His Ipswich mills prospered for many years making tubular stockings for men and women to wear beneath their trousers and long skirts. In the 1920s, however, the fashion of short skirts destroyed the business and the machinery was sold to Russia in 1928. For a time a new company that used flatbed knitters to make full-fashioned silk stockings continued Ipswich's industrial tradition.[22]

Lawrence's mill, however, was sold to Sylvania Electric of Lynn, which made fuses for artillery shells here during World War II. Now the old mill has been spruced up by an information-age concern, EBSCO Publishing Company. Its employees are readers who abstract periodicals to supply on-line reference service to libraries and other subscribers. The town plans to build a river walk to connect the mills and the village stores and restaurants at the end of the millpond.[23]

Ipswich is a white town whose population is estimated to be 13,000. A few of the residents are African American, Asian, or Hispanic. Greeks, who have concentrated in the clam business, and a Polish community add a bit of ethnic color to the local culture. In terms of income, Ipswich lies within the Boston region's comfort zone; its resident households' median income ($42,386, in 1989 dollars) resembles that of the western towns of Framingham, Natick, and Marlborough. And like most towns it has its invisible poor. In the 1990 census, 630 persons were reported as living below the poverty line, people who, whatever their plight, are not numerous enough to attract public or political notice.[24]

In the past century, Ipswich land has enjoyed several moments of good fortune. During the nineteenth and early twentieth centuries it attracted gentlemen's farms and extensive vacation spreads. The presence of such families fostered a preservation ethic, both for saving and restoring old houses and for tending a gardened and pastoral landscape. In 1909 a Chicago plumbing millionaire, Richard T. Crane, Jr. (1873–1931), purchased 500 acres of drumlin and beach called Castle Hill, so named because it was intended to be the site for a fort during the seventeenth century. On this property he constructed a great house, outbuildings, and gardens and continued to purchase land until his holdings totaled 3,500 acres. (The current great house is the second on the site; the first was torn down and replaced by this one in 1928.) In time the Crane family settled in Ipswich, and in 1945 family members turned over 1,000 acres of dunes and beach to the Trustees of the Reservations. When Mrs. Crane died, the drumlin and its great house were deeded to the trustees, and in 1957 the son's wife added a 650-acre wildlife refuge to the trustees' holdings.[25] Others have followed the Cranes' example. In 1998 the Appleton Farm of 500 acres along Route 1A was transferred to the trustees, as has the Greenwood Farm of one hundred acres at the edge of the Great Marsh.

Recently an unexpected turn of events has also contributed to the preservation of Ipswich's pastoral look. During the decades of depression and war several Catholic orders purchased private estates. Now, as the members of these orders have grown fewer and older the large houses and grounds are again up for sale. In response the town has created a special Great Estate Preservation Development Use Zone to work with the purchasers of these large parcels. The general approach is to approve plans for clusters of houses or offices in return for commitments to preserve the old buildings and fields.[26]

As things stand, ordinary incremental development is probably more of a threat to the town's existing landscapes than is the development of a few large parcels. The town has been growing at a rate of 1 percent per year (or about fifty building permits for new houses). Were current zoning regulations to be left in place and all the land developed accordingly, the town would almost double to have a built-out population of 23,000. As is common in Boston's towns, the land yet to be developed is zoned for one acre per dwelling, a pattern that destroys fields and all broad views. Ipswich is considering some sort of roadside zoning overlay to protect the looks of its major roads, and it has established a growth management committee to explore whether future growth can follow patterns that will preserve the qualities of the town. In 1999 this committee, whose members include many concerned with building and land development, decided to hold public meetings to discern whether some sort of consensus exists in the town about what its images are and which ones residents wish to preserve.[27]

The precedents are not all favorable. On one of the town's most attractive sites, another drumlin (the Neck), which overlooks the Great Marsh and the barrier Plum Island State Park and Parker River National Refuge, summer people have crowded small cottages along the ridge to catch the views and the cool summer breezes. In these prosperous times, families are modernizing their cottages and others are reworking them so they may be all-year-round residences. As additions press upward and outward, the Neck families block views from right, left, and above. The look of this rebuilding seaside community recalls the antics of a crowd of penguins who gather at the ocean's edge, pushing and shoving until one falls into the sea, either to be eaten by a waiting seal or to signal to the others that it is safe to fish.

On the Neck the problem is not seals but sewerage. The houses are served by town water, but each small lot must contain its own septic system. If these are neglected, the contamination seeps onto the tidal clam beds nearby. An entire new sewer system will be very expensive. Only the central village of Ipswich is now sewered. The Neck and the town are hoping to avoid this necessity by close inspection. Whatever the outcome, the Neck stands as a warning about what an unregulated land market can do.

Preservation, farming, and clamming, no matter how intelligently pursued, do not by themselves establish a sustainable urban environmental policy. Nowhere does this truth carry more force than in Ipswich's relationships to the larger region served by the Ipswich River. Here past law and past practices haunt the present, and the potpourri of local initiatives cannot sustain the river or its basin.

The Ipswich River flows twenty-four miles from its source in the wetlands of Wilmington and Middleton out to the sea at Ipswich. Three hundred and thirty-five thousand residents in fourteen cities and towns draw their daily water from the river. Current withdrawals exceed capacity. Possibilities for the recharge of the flow are lost because 80 percent of the water taken goes to cities and towns that export it out of the Ipswich Basin via waste treatment plants that discharge elsewhere (Beverly, Burlington, Danvers, Lynn, Peabody, Salem, Reading, and Wilmington). Here too, as throughout the Boston city region, old broken-joint sewer lines draw millions of gallons of ground water from the surrounding water table. As a consequence of these exports, when there is a drought, as in 1999, the river stops flowing. In more extreme times, as in 1995 and 1997, it dried up to such a degree that observers could walk the streambed without getting their feet wet. The river's problems are intensified by the conditions of the underlying land. In the 155-square-mile drainage basin the aquifers are small and fragmented. The great sand and gravel beds of the western and southern parts of the Boston region do not exist here. Instead, ledge and glacial till make it hard to initiate a runoff and septic field recharge program such as exists in some other towns.[28]

These physical problems intensify other failings. The traditional water law of Massachusetts provides no mechanism to adjudicate conflicts over the withdrawal of ground water, as opposed to the running water of rivers and lakes. Thus, town wells lie beyond the common law's reach.[29] This old legal tradition mocks common sense because most of the water in any river basin rests in the ground, not on the surface. To remedy this legal deficiency the Massachusetts Department of Environmental Protection has been authorized to license major withdrawals. In the case of the Ipswich River, however, it has issued more licenses than there is water. It did so by grandfathering past withdrawal rates. Amidst this confusion, each town follows its own practice. Some have become effective in fixing leaking water pipes; others have installed accurate meters; still others teach conservation. The town of Wareham has even instituted a rate structure that encourages water saving by making the per-gallon charges rise with use. In 1999, Ipswich itself withdrew one and a half times its licensed quantity of water.

Many remedies suggest themselves: repair more sewers and

water lines, upgrade all the water meters, establish progressive rate structures to discourage waste and summer use, reconfigure some sewage treatment plants so that they can discharge back into the Basin. Yet, most immediately, what is missing is some organization with the responsibility and power to oversee the river basin and to plan for its management in the context of the basin's inevitable population growth. The links among highways, shopping malls and strips, industrial parks, and incremental residential development have yet to come forcibly into public and political consciousness. Yet clean water and a river of running water are essentials for the maintenance of the congeries of ecosystems that make healthy human life possible.[30]

LAWRENCE

Although rows of massive brick mill buildings as large as today's downtown skyscrapers form the spine of this city, Lawrence does not rise up in the region's horizon, either visually or in its imagination. The mills and the acres of close-packed wooden houses that are home to seventy thousand rest in a valley along the course of the Merrimack River, so that when you drive along I-495 the road offers only a brief glimpse of the city as it crosses over the river.

More masks hide Lawrence from the region than the mere screening of the hills between the freeway and the city. Lawrence is one of the poor companions that journey with the nation's and the Boston region's successive transformations. Most of its processes of poverty remain unseen because they take place beyond the gaze of the important and the powerful or the curiosity of journalists and politicians. Poverty is something that families experience and recall, but it is not a history most wish to parade. Of course, the cause of poverty varies according to local circumstances. Sometimes it comes from companies closing up, sometimes from a purchaser carrying off a local business to another location; sometimes too many have lined up for too few jobs, or the crowd offering to work is so numerous that employers don't have to pay livable wages.

All of these conditions and more have combined to settle poverty upon the core cities of the Boston region. At the region's center, African American and Hispanic poverty are the examples journalists and politicians speak about. But poverty elsewhere is not news, even though as many poor live in the mill towns that ring the region as in the center. Lawrence's 27 percent rate of poverty among its residents was not news, but Boston's 18 percent was. More invisible still are the thousands who live scattered through the suburbs and towns everywhere. Throughout the region food pantries attempt to supplement family diets by providing free food. There are at least 850 locations in operation because, as one director put it, "We are dealing with a lot of working-class poor who are earning $7 and $8 an hour and, after paying the light bill and rent, have nothing for food."[31]

Some of the region's poverty is the product of fathers abandoning their children, and of failure to provide old people with sufficient healthcare and Social Security benefits, but much of the region's current poverty is the consequence of migration: the outflow of businesses that have sought cheap labor or have been bought up by outside corporations, and, contrarywise, the inflow of young immigrants who have sought homes in a region of high employment. Because these newcomers often lack mastery of the English language or skills to match their employers' essential needs, they have not been able to demand decent wages.[32]

In Lawrence immigration and poverty are a familiar story, now, once again, being acted out by new people in a new economy. But, as always, what happens next door and within the city is often the consequence of events taking place far beyond the reach of local people.

Lawrence itself was the overnight creation of nonresident textile magnates. The city's current development director likes to refer

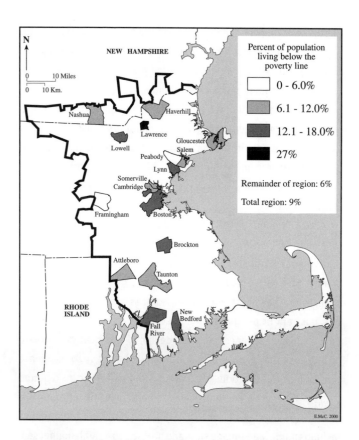

Map 12. Percentage of Population Living Below the Poverty Line in Central Boston Cities and Old Mill Towns

to it as the nation's first industrial park. The Essex Corporation of nearby Lowell petitioned the legislature to set off a seven-and-a-half-square-mile tract from the towns of Andover and Methuen in order to establish a separate town. During the years 1845 and 1846 Abbott Lawrence (1792–1855), brother of William Lawrence, the pioneer textile investor, laid out and built this new factory town. The flight of Irish laborers from the famine on their island supplied a large pool of labor to build a granite dam across the Merrimack, dig the water power canals, and raise the brick factories. The corporation also laid out a seventeen-acre common in the center of town, but this gift ended its residential planning. In time the little wooden houses and tenements common to the region and era replaced the construction workers' shacks, and a conventional Boston mill town emerged: immigrants and laborers crowded together on the flats next to the mills, the mechanics, foremen, supervisors, and storekeepers on the surrounding hills, and the corporate officers and stockholders in Boston and Brookline or some other comfortable remove.[33]

A second boom swept the town during the early twentieth century when William Wood assembled a number of formerly independent companies into his giant American Woolen Company, a worsted spinner and weaver. One of his great new mills, the Ayer Mill of 1905, is now having its clock tower restored to stand as a reminder of a past era of prosperity. It can serve as an ephemeral symbol only, because Lawrence had been designed and built to a pattern of business that grew ever more outmoded after 1920. Lawrence was a long-run, big production place. So long as Americans required yards of blue, gray, and brown worsted and miles of cotton prints, its strategies proved efficient. Once department stores and women's fashions made ready-made suits and dresses quickly changing, seasonal fashion items, American Woolen and its cotton equivalents became beached whales. From the postwar price collapse of 1921 on through the 1950s the textile firms of the Boston region struggled on, only to finally collapse after the end of the World War II and the Korean War military orders. Hard times set in at Lawrence in 1953.[34]

Strange, unexpected political and cultural crosscurrents also hastened the city's decline. In the 1890s, national politicians like Theodore Roosevelt swept the nation into imperial adventures, most particularly the seizure of the Spanish empire in the Caribbean and the Pacific. American troops invaded Puerto Rico and made the island a protectorate, thereby linking these islanders to the mainland. A few years later, from 1916 to 1924, U.S. troops occupied the Dominican Republic to force that island's government to pay its debts to international bankers. Later in 1965 the island was again occupied out of fear that its citizens might fall under the influence of Fidel Castro. At the time of their instigation, none of these imperial events seemed to portend new peoples or new ways for the United States, and surely Lawrence was an unimaginable connection. Yet invasion brought knowledge of the States to islanders, and in time migration and ties.

During these very same decades when Americans cheered for empire, many also grew fearful of the very nation that they had made. The year 1910 marked a peak year for overseas immigration. A fearful nativism swept the nation, in part abetted by labor unions who wanted to reduce the influx of cheap labor. New England and Boston took a leading role in the immigration restriction demands. Wartime xenophobia and the subsequent Red Scare added further impetus to the restrictive campaign. The 1921 and 1924 federal laws stopped down the migratory flow. Of course Lawrence, which re-quired an army of machine tenders, had always been an immigrant town, first English and Irish, then Italian, French Canadian, Greek, and Syrian. Low wage, youthful immigrant labor was the very energy that had made the machinery profitable. Now the flow was stopped. Textile manufacturers in the Boston region and nearby accelerated their migration to the south and west, where they sought nonunion, underemployed rural men and women. The mills that remained and prospered in Lawrence and the Boston region developed new ways. Like Lawrence's Malden Mills, they formed close, quick service re-lationships with their customers, they kept purchasing the latest machinery, and they invested heavily in research and development. Today the well-known Polartec of the Malden Mills is manufactured in a union shop.

As new economic arrangements closed down Lawrence's manu-facturing, so did similar events drastically reduce manufacturing in

Old Power Canal, Lawrence

New York City. Across the nation, manufacturing moved to the metro-politan fringes or the Sun Belt. Thereby old mill towns and New York became reservoirs of cheap housing, and also places of opportu-nity for those willing to work in services. Puerto Ricans flooded into New York City to take the places of the children and grandchildren of immigrants who had formerly tended its factories. Then, beginning in the 1960s, and especially after the assassination of the dictator Rafael Trujillo, the Dominicans followed the Puerto Ricans into New York.[35] By 1970 thousands of Puerto Ricans had found their way to Lawrence, and later, in the 1980s, they flooded in, joined this time by Dominican immigrants. The 1990 census reported that Lawrence had become, once again, an immigrant city, this time a Latino one, with 15,000 Puerto Ricans and 11,000 Dominicans.[36]

Today, Lawrence is not an easy place. Old-timers, the children and grandchildren of Lawrence immigrants, will tell you that Law-rence is not the same as it was. Some will say the Hispanics have ruined it. Surely it is not the same as its pre–World War I peak, when 20,000 workers streamed through the mill gates, or the Indus-trial Workers of the World organized across ethnic prejudices to carry off the successful Bread and Roses strike. In 1999, there were only 6,500 manufacturing jobs within the city.[37] Unemployment runs double the state average, and perhaps a third of the residents make their way with income below the federal government's inappropri-ately low poverty line.[38] Household incomes are so low that the main street (Essex Street) has lost most of its stores and the *Lawrence Eagle-Tribune*, the city's daily newspaper, has removed its reporters and plant to North Andover. Outbound textile companies, when they abandoned their properties, left behind massive pollution problems for the city to clean up. Lawrence also suffers all the pains of a high crime rate; in 1997, violence and robbery were more severe than in all of central Boston except Chelsea.[39]

As in poor neighborhoods everywhere, local wages will not sus-tain rents for an adequate maintenance of many buildings. Since the 1950s, Lawrence's comfortable families have been moving out of town to nearby Methuen and Haverhill and suburbs in southern New Hampshire. Lawrence's public schools have not been well managed; indeed, a few years ago the state put them in receivership. Such social and economic trends conjoin to encourage landlords to stop paying taxes, even to burn down and abandon their properties. Some observers have estimated that there are fifteen hundred vacant lots and tax-delinquent properties in the city. Such a weak real estate market saps the city's fiscal power so that it does not dare to enact "living wage" legislation to require city contractors and development beneficiaries to pay more than minimum wages to their employees. Boston, by contrast, started such a program in 1997.[40] A recent report by the U.S. Department of Housing and Urban Development listed Lawrence with New York City and Newark as cities with overstrained public services and local economies that had yet to catch the wave of high-tech prosperity.[41]

A good deal of the city's difficulty comes from having all its land built upon. Unlike its upstream neighbor, Nashua, there are not large open spaces on which to locate new industrial parks, malls, or residential subdivisions. Here modernization means tearing down or rehabilitating. The city's development director, William Luster, thinks that the best way to refashion the old mill clusters is to tear down some mills to make way for parking and good truck access. One such cluster, the River Walk, after a painful beginning, has been developed successfully in this pattern, and there are hopes for more. The city's basic development strategy, since it does not own any mills, is to seek government grants so that it can offer special services and tax incentives to any employers who might wish to come to town.[42]

On its own account, Lawrence can offer an abundance of men and women who are willing to work hard. The pool of young immigrants is its greatest asset, and it is through them that the city is taking its place in the Boston region's economy. As always in the past, the immigrants are not the poorest of their homelands. They are people of some education and some connections that enable them to make their way from the Caribbean to New York City and on to Lawrence. When they arrive here their skills and education count for little because they have not yet mastered English. The first step, thus, is to report to the temporary employment agencies, unless a relative has secured a job for them. As temps, the beginners travel out from the city in vans to the nearby industrial parks and malls to do all manner of laborer and building care jobs. They pack products into boxes, load trucks, assemble stuff, clean and sweep, cook, sew, and wash. At night they crowd into oversubscribed English as a Second Language classes. In time, as their English grows, these young people find stable niches in the region's manufacturing plants and in the many small Latino businesses that have started to spring up.

In this human progress the key resource is family. The gatherings of relatives and the helping networks of brothers, sisters, aunts and uncles, cousins, and parents are essential for survival. These ties allow the sharing of houses and apartments so that each person's rent can be kept low enough to permit remittances to be sent back to the islands. The same ties allow the immigrant to escape the uncertain and ill-paid work of the temporary agencies. Dominicans and Puerto Ricans pride themselves on the warmth and inclusiveness of their families, but like others who have preceded them, family is not an easy institution to maintain in the face of the inevitable conflicts between the immigrant generation and their American-born children.[43]

Many social clubs and churches are trying to assist immigrants in their adaptation. One, in particular, is trying to foster a self-helping neighborhood by combining some of the old programs of settlement houses with the newer functions of residential reconstruction. The Lawrence Planning and Neighborhood Development Corporation has assumed responsibility for a couple of dozen blocks in the northeast corner of the downtown. North Common, as it is called, is the oldest residential area in the city, a cluster of three-deckers and six-flats that has long served as the port of entry to the city's newest immigrants. As a community development corporation it has built some housing, and it looks forward to several more physical improvement tasks. It wants to assemble vacant and tax-delinquent properties to make playgrounds and to find federal funds for housing rehabilitation. Its most ambitious and significant goal, however, is its current campaign to build and operate an educational center.

The location for the proposed Gateway Family Learning Center is the product of earlier white flight. The former social and cultural center of the North Common neighborhood, the church of St. Laurence O'Toole, was torn down in 1980 by the archdiocese. In addition the Augustinian Brothers, who had managed a social service agency there, retreated to their college, Merrimack College, in North Andover. They continue to own the parish house and land where St. Laurence stood. Here, on the historic base of the neighborhood, director Bill Traynor and the neighborhood residents propose to build and run their educational center. Lifelong learning, a mirror of the very path of immigrants, will be the organizing theme. For young mothers the center hopes to establish a combined day care and mothers' support program, for children many after-school activities in art, music, tutoring, and study hall, and for adults English as a second language, job training, and whatever general education the neighborhood demands.[44]

At present the power and effectiveness of the development corporation rests on its skilled staff and its alliance with an active neighborhood association of residents. Also, the Augustinians have agreed to return and to have their students and faculty assist in the educational offerings. The next step is, as always, the securing of grants to build the center, lay out the playgrounds, refurbish the houses. It remains to be seen how local, state, and national administrators and politicians will respond. It is now up to them to either nurture or disdain the very human processes that have built the Boston region since 1620.

METRO WEST: FRAMINGHAM AND NATICK

Directly west of Boston, parallel to the old railroad (1835), Massachusetts Route 9 (paved 1931), and the newer Massachusetts Turnpike (1957), there lies a cluster of eight suburban and mill towns that have assumed the collective name of Metro West. The *Middlesex News* of Framingham invented the term in 1983, and since then the paper and the Chamber of Commerce have successfully promoted it. Now there is even a growth and development committee of this name that tries to deal with the group as a whole.[45] The inventors and users of the label want to stress the independence of the area from central Boston (table 4).

The eight towns are, however, hardly independent. They are deeply enmeshed in the living and working patterns of the new Boston regional society and its economy. Weston and Wellesley took their present form after World War I to serve rail commuters to downtown Boston. Rural Wayland and Sudbury remade themselves as automobile bedroom towns after World War II. Ashland, a former mill town, now functions as a Framingham and I-495 suburb, while Natick, Framingham, and Marlborough are old manufacturing towns, cogs in the nineteenth-century clustering of Boston's regional specialties. Like all Boston-area towns, Natick, Framingham, and Marlborough have suffered from the obsolescence of their industries, from buyouts and mill closings. For instance, the Dennison Manufacturing Company was lured from Maine in 1897 and for the next century flourished as Framingham's largest employer. Begun with a fresh idea for making shipping tags, the business expanded into all manner of stationery goods until it was bought out by a national corporation in February 1998. In 1948 the General Mo-

Towns East to West	Population 1995	Median Household Income 1989–90	Foreign-Born 1990	Below Poverty Line 1989–90
Wellesley	28,100	$79,000	2,342	985
Weston	12,200	95,000	859	367
Natick	31,000	49,000	2,046	947
Wayland	12,600	49,000	974	202
Framingham	64,700	43,000	7,604	3,444
Sudbury	15,600	79,000	1,005	215
Ashland	13,400	51,000	808	229
Marlborough	33,400	41,000	2,831	1,183
Total	211,000		18,469	7,572

SOURCES: U.S. Bureau of the Census, *1990 Census of Population, Social and Economic Characteristics, Massachusetts* (Washington, D.C.: Government Printing Office, September 1993), sec. 1, tables 1, 3; *Metropolitan Area Community Profiles* (Boston: MAPC, 1998).

NOTE: The Metro West Growth Management Committee of the Metropolitan Area Planning Council includes the Worcester County town of Southborough (population 6,700 in 1990), which lies outside the study area of this book.

tors Corporation opened a large assembly plant on the south side of Framingham that employed 4,000 workers at high union wages. The plant closed in 1989.[46] In the 1970s, Metro West boomed with plants making small and midsized computers, only to have that specialty fade from the competition with personal computers. Thousands of jobs disappeared in the late 1980s and early 1990s.[47] Unlike more peripheral mill towns like Lawrence and New Bedford, however, here the location along the main east-west axis of the region's economy, halfway between the state's two largest cities, Boston and Worcester, has given these places a resiliency that others have lacked. All the towns are labor importers; inbound commuters arrive daily to staff the Metro West services, stores, and manufacturing plants.[48]

Today's daily traffic, which reaches as far as southern New Hampshire, offers a nice contrast between new and old. During the first two decades of the twentieth century, the many mills of Metro West drew their labor across a cluster of nineteen western towns. The means of travel was a crisscross of interurban railroads that linked one rural mill village to the next. Small companies operated this service with a few cars that shuttled back and forth once, twice, or three times an hour. Workers and shoppers had to plan their trips by the trolleys' schedules. What with the walk to the stop, the ride, and the walk at the other end, the average commute probably took an hour. Later in the day housewives would use the cars to shop in local centers like Framingham and Waltham. Today the average commuting time is about twenty-three minutes, but to use the you-go-when-you-want road system commuters must make payments on, or own, a car and keep the gas tank filled. Progress here in Boston always speaks with a forked tongue.[49]

Charles River, South Natick

Of all the towns in the Metro West area, Framingham and Natick are the most significant because they display in easy plenitude the commonplace patterns of contemporary Boston and the United States. Here affordable housing tracts, automobile living, new immigrants, shopping malls, industrial parks, and emptied Main Streets abound. These two towns also demonstrate some important initiatives for coping with the recent patterns. Both are as creative and innovative as they are because their local governments are buoyed by steady revenues from highway-oriented industrial parks and shopping malls located within their boundaries.

Framingham

In Framingham the old Worcester Turnpike (Massachusetts Route 9) serves as the social watershed. The north side is prosperous, the south side modest or poor. The town's historic center lies on the north, and here too are found the 1950s and 1960s tract houses that have recently quadrupled in value. On the far northern edge, next to Wayland and Sudbury, there is open land zoned for one-acre parcels, and there are expensive homes.

An industrial park and a continuous strip of stores and malls line the turnpike itself. This strip runs on to the east through neighboring Natick. Here, on seventy acres, stood the pioneering Shoppers' World of 1951, now torn down and rebuilt.[50] Framingham is also headquarters to such successful national firms as T.J. Maxx, Staples, and Bose. Their offices, warehouses, and plants are now joined by biotech firms.

In 1834 the Boston and Worcester Railroad planned to run its tracks next to the then–town center, but stagecoach and tavern operators opposed the new competitor's route. They forced the railroad to an alternative location, two miles to the south. Here the railroad lines and station have become Framingham's center.[51] The closing of the General Motors plant and the buyout and severe cutback of the Dennison Manufacturing Company, two big southside employers, and the Route 9 competition emptied out the town's railroad center at Union, Concord, and Hollis streets. Optimists, however, envision fresh possibilities for the now-vacant and underutilized stores. The town's building inspector, Lewis Colten, a former architect and planner, imagines a changed function for the big mall stores. He expects that they will become something like a warehouse open to any of the public who might choose to come. There the shoppers would roam the aisles among the store's pickers, who would be rushing about filling orders that had been placed over the Internet. In such a future, the town center would be taken up afresh by small specialty shops and services, places where personalized attention could be offered once again. As of 1997, two shoe stores that offer careful fitting, shoe dyeing, and fits for difficult feet exemplify this kind of future.[52]

An abundance of cheap labor stands as an essential precondition to such a retail future. Framingham has a gold mine of such: 5,000 Hispanic and 2,000 Asian immigrants. These latest migrants continue the town's long population history of newcomers arriving to find some opportunity. First came the Yankees and the Irish to work in the textile mills along the Sudbury River and to build the railroads. Then came the French Canadians and Italians to work in Dennison's tag factory. Many of the Italians also began as stonecutters, imported to help build the nearby reservoir dams of the metropolitan water system. Eastern European Jews came also to sew in the cap factory and other shops. After World War II a large nursery, Wyman's Garden Center, imported Puerto Ricans. Indian and Chinese technicians followed to staff the computer plants of Digital and Data General. The 1970s also saw the arrival of Russian Jews fleeing yet another wave of anti-Semitism there. In the mid-1980s the Brazilians began to arrive. Many think Framingham and neighboring Marlborough became their destination because Portuguese shoe workers had been imported years ago to work in the local factories. In addition, Framingham is home to an African American community of 2,000. It is a middle-class settlement whose most famous resident to date has been Solomon Carter Fuller, the psychiatrist.[53]

One author has characterized Framingham as "the northernmost town in Brazil," and he estimated that there might be 12,000 Brazilians in the Framingham-Marlborough area. These latest immigrants do not occupy the manufacturing niche others have filled. Instead, they have developed specialties in housecleaning, child care, and landscape work, all of which are made profitable by family teams working long hours.

The Brazilian migratory pattern repeats the ways of earlier immigrants. Framingham's Brazilians are well-educated, reasonably well-off small-town folks who travel to the provincial city of Governador Valadares to make their way to the United States. This city is in the heart of a mining, iron, and steel province (Minas Gerais) about two hundred miles north of Rio de Janeiro. Brazilian inflation, and the knowledge that their labor would be worth twice as much in the United States as in Brazil, seem to have started the migration in 1985. A typical *brazuca* arrives on a tourist visa and begins washing dishes in restaurants or making beds in motels. The editor of Governador Valadares' immigrant newspaper, a journal that features Framingham as well as Brazilian advertisements, began her career as a worker at McDonald's on Route 9.

The first major step to indepedence comes when the newcomer has mastered enough English to pass the Massachusetts driver's license test. This license, which contains a Social Security number, serves as a sort of minimum requirement of proper working papers for many of the region's employers. Under present laws most of the Brazilians are illegal migrants. Unlike the Puerto Ricans, who can shuttle back and forth to their island, the Brazilians find it hard to return. They do send their American-born children back and forth, sometimes for a Brazilian education. In addition to the usual networks of relatives, St. Tarcinius Church in Framingham serves as an important social center. Here jobs can be found, and help summoned if the Immigration and Naturalization Service picks someone up.

Because theirs is a self-helping entrepreneurial community, the Brazilians enjoy a good local reputation. In their illegal status, however, they do present some problems for the town. On the one hand, they do not add to the welfare rolls, but on the other hand their children must be educated, and no taxes can be assessed until Brazilians become property owners. Absent any change in immigration laws, it seems likely that this fiscal problem will disappear as soon as the American-born generation comes of age.[54]

Framingham's housing has been pulled in opposing directions. Plant closings have brought some southside housing abandonment. In contrast, the arrival of immigrants has forced much doubling up so that the newcomers can make the rent payments. These contrary tendencies have thereby furnished opportunities for unscrupulous landlords to either temporarily abandon their property or siphon off rents without regard to conditions within their buildings or concern for their behavior's effect on the neighborhood. Building Inspector Lewis Colten has invented a uniquely effective method to discipline such offenders. Like the Puritans before him, his weapon is shame. If a landlord does not respond to repeated notices of violations, Colten institutes condemnation proceedings and simultaneously sends his crew to board up the house with bright red sheets of plywood. He then hangs a banner in front, next to the sidewalk, that reads: "The owner of this property chooses not to cooperate with town officials and has created a blight and nuisance in our neighborhood." Beside this message, in big letters, appears the owner's name, and often the telephone number as well. Conditions that have frustrated neighbors and city officials elsewhere, have, thanks to Colten's medicine, found a quick remedy here. He also coordinates his boarding up with the police when they raid a drug house. As an approving resident said, "We all felt we didn't want to see the largest investment we've ever made go down the tubes."[55]

Natick

Natick, Framingham's eastern neighbor, shares many of the larger town's characteristics: acres of modest ranch and Cape-style tract homes of the 1950s and 1960s, many immigrants, but here predominantly Puerto Rican, prosperous malls on Route 9, old mills along the river, and a southern edge next to Wellesley, Dover, and Sherborn for one-acre lots and the building of expensive homes. Like Framingham, too, the schools are good. Sports are especially emphasized here. Natick is one of the Boston region's several towns that identify themselves as the home of "champions."

In these times of rapid urban decentralization, Natick's environmental efforts recommend it to towns everywhere. The city of Boston's first reservoir, Lake Cochituate and its associated ponds, cut through the center of Natick from north to south. These are important elements in the Sudbury-Concord River drainage basin. Further, the southeast corner of town abuts the Charles River. Thus, at least half of Natick lies upon or drains into the aquifers of these valuable urban water resources, and the town itself draws its drinking water from wells in the two basins.

In the post–World War II boom, a local contractor ran up hundreds of small ranch houses and Capes on concrete slabs. Because the houses lacked basements, the oil tanks for the furnaces were buried in the ground nearby. Twenty years later these tanks had rusted, and they began to leak into the aquifers. The town successfully applied to the U.S. Department of Housing and Urban Development for a grant of a million dollars, and it issued bonds to the same amount. With this fund, plus homeowner's fees that ran from $5,000 to $15,000, it removed 350 oil tanks and their surrounding polluted ground. Now the town has established aquifer protection zoning over these drainage areas. In these new zones, storm runoff from houses must run directly onto the ground or into dry wells to recharge the underlying aquifer. Commercial parking lots in turn

1740s Prototype Cape Cod Houses, Yarmouthport

must filter their runoff before returning it to the ground. The town has also capped its former dump, and, in cooperation with neighboring Sherborn, will open an eighteen-hole golf course on top of the buried trash.[56]

These public works and regulatory efforts have been accompanied by an innovative educational program managed jointly by the Natick Department of Recreation and Human Services, the School Department, and an independent board. The Natick Community Farm now operates a twenty-two-acre organic farm next to the Memorial Elementary School in South Natick, and its staff teach farm, gardening, and environmental material throughout the Natick schools. The farm began in 1974 in imitation of Bill McElwain's Green Power project in nearby Weston. Over the ensuing years it has matured from a summer youth program to a year-round educational institution. In addition to teaching Natick children, the farm runs a work program for Down's syndrome children and for women in drug recovery. The director, Lynda Simkins, likes to say, "At this farm we keep an open gate." To help with its budget the farm operates a popular vegetable stand and sells maple syrup, turkeys, eggs, meat,

1950s Cape-style Houses, Natick

and live rabbits. Its many activities with volunteers, schools, and supporters serve the town at large by keeping voters' attention on the issues of good environmental management.[57]

The Natick shopping malls, part of the Framingham-Natick "Golden Triangle," are tied to Natick's town center program like partners in a difficult marriage. Both must be maintained and both must succeed. The shops on Route 9 drained the business from the town center at Central and Main streets, yet the mall stores deliver each year about $2.5 million in tax revenues to the town. Town planners are concerned that fragmented ownership might result in deficient overall maintenance of the lucrative strip. They are also aware that amenity standards for malls and their parking lots have been rising since the 1960s. Therefore, to promote modernization and some coordination of signage they have instituted a mall overlay zone that requires any owner who requests a permit for some building change to combine the request with improvements to match the new exterior standards. So far little change is apparent, but the long-run goal of continuing modernization seems a wise one. Natick also maintains a single tax policy so that commercial properties pay at the same rate as residences. The benefit of this policy is two-fold. Uniformity makes business people feel that they are not being singled out as cash cows by the town meeting. It also saves the town the endlessly conflicting results of special tax cuts and moratoria given to attract new businesses. Such maneuvering frequently drains the revenues of cities and towns with differential rates, places like the city of Boston.

The mall revenues have financed a municipal rebuilding program at the town center. So far Natick has erected a new government row: the library received a handsome large addition, a new firehouse and police station went up, and more recently a new town hall was built. Altogether these four compose an attractive street front, well in keeping with the nineteenth-century blocks nearby on Main Street. Negotiations are also under way with the MBTA to build a parking garage next to the downtown train station so that rail commuters might be encouraged and might linger longer in the center of town.

Natick also enjoys the luck of being the home of a tireless music promoter, Michael Moran. Moran began by booking folk singers in nearby coffeehouses in 1992, and since then he has expanded his goals to envision Natick as a center for the arts, especially music. He wants to have all sorts of music: classical, jazz, folk, and dance theater. Moran holds to a very important social truth. As he puts it, "Through the popular arts people meet and come to accept each other." He also takes encouragement from the success of other suburban music clubs like the Old Vienna in Westborough, which ran folk, rock, and jazz, two shows a night, five nights a week, for ten

Taunton River at the Berkley-Dighton Bridge

years. Since 1998 Moran has been operating an art gallery and music program in temporary quarters on Main Street. He and his supporters now hope to find a permanent home in a redundant firehouse just off Main Street.[58]

So far the town has lured three restaurants to the old center, and a very popular bakery has opened next to the green. It remains to be seen whether or not Natick or Framingham can find the right recipes for a sustained town center restoration in an era so dominated by automobiles. At least the two have the resources to experiment.

THE VISION 2020 INITIATIVE

The most ambitious of all the planning and growth management programs in the Boston city region is now unfolding in the boom town area of southeastern Massachusetts (Bristol and Plymouth counties). This broad area has been changing according to three different patterns. The shore towns have been rapidly piling up summer cottages and retirement homes since the completion during the 1960s of State Route 3 as a freeway and the extension of I-495 to the edge of Cape Cod. At the same time, industrial obsolescence and the destruction of the fisheries have visited economic depression on the region's cities of New Bedford, Fall River, Taunton, and Brockton. Elsewhere, from the northern edge of towns serving as Boston suburbs and extending south to Rhode Island and Buzzards Bay, towns have prospered with the new highway access. Even Taunton and Brockton, both of which were suffering from the loss of old industries, were able to grow because they possessed open land near interchanges where they located malls and industrial parks. The most ubiquitous forms of new growth have been the mixed roadside commercial and residential strip and the small patch residential subdivision. According to planner Steven Smith, more land has been taken up for development since 1950 than in all the preceding three hundred years (table 5).[59]

To date, these commonplace additions have proven destructive to the towns and the region. Southeastern Massachusetts is Boston's "Lakes District," a landscape of ponds, wetlands, and cranberry bogs. Indeed, until recent Wisconsin and Oregon competi-

TABLE FIVE   Vision 2020 Area of Southeastern Massachusetts

| | Population | | Change | |
Cities	1950	1990	Number	Percentage
Attleboro	23,809	38,383	14,574	61
Brockton	62,860	92,788	29,928	48
Fall River	111,163	92,703	−18,460	−17
New Bedford	109,189	99,992	−9,197	−8
Plymouth	13,608	45,608	32,000	235
Taunton	40,109	49,832	9,723	24
All 2020 Towns	602,525	941,601	339,076	56

tion, here stood the cranberry capital of the world. There are towns in this area half of whose land is wetlands. Thus, whatever runs into the brooks and marshes quickly percolates through the glacial sands. The example of Otis Air National Guard Base and Camp Edwards on nearby Cape Cod stands as a fearful warning. The military dumped thousands of gallons of fuel and heaps of heavy metals on the grounds of their reservation. The mess now percolates in an ever-expanding plume, threatening the water supply of near towns. After years of clean-up effort and study, a plan, which is likely to be carried out, proposes that two-thirds of the reservation become a wildlife and fresh-water protection area.[60]

Visitors and residents alike are drawn to the region by two strong attractions: the ocean shore and the pastoral towns of old village centers and surrounding fields. The quality of the shore depends upon the accidents of geology and the behavior of the beachside residents. Some towns, like Duxbury, have inherited a beautiful barrier beach which is maintained as a town beach, an exclusive amenity for town residents. Others, like Scituate, present a shoreline disfigured by a continuous line of houses. In general, however, the comparative wealth of shoreline residents, summer and year-round people, means a high level of gardening and maintenance — and often, too, historic preservation districts and environmentally active birders and sportsmen.

The interior does not share this culture of wealth. Instead, most towns have been places of modest living, even poverty, where growth and land profits have required patient waiting. Here a retail strip means a chance for a farmer or an odd-lot owner to cash out. Bit by bit the intertown roads have been attracting houses, subdivisions, restaurants, auto shops, contractor's yards, and little stores and services of all kinds. Some of these roads are now clogged with traffic, and when that happens the owners and residents call for the state to widen the road to make it safe. Of course, once widened at considerable expense, more retail activity follows until the situation repeats itself. Such fringe development, which supplements the offerings of the malls, combines with the new malls to destroy old town centers as gathering and shopping places. The malls, of course, settle down next to the highway interchanges, thereby fattening one town and beggaring its neighbor. So, Taunton got the Silver City Mall and $1.5 million in new tax revenues, while neighboring Berkley got only the traffic.[61]

Currently the most destructive development practices have their origin in the tax policies of the commonwealth. State laws have built a municipal fight ring in which everyone is getting badly hurt. Fiscal concerns are driving land-use decisions. For instance, the state offers to pay 59 percent of the cost of new school construction but nothing for remodeling existing schools. Inappropriately large new elementary and middle schools thus replace smaller old neighborhood ones. High schools, often formerly located for convenience at the center of town, now migrate to edge campuses, which can be reached only by car or bus. Many of the planners in these towns would like to propose adding modest housing on small lots near the existing village centers, but no such innovation can pass a town meeting because such a policy would allow building homes that would attract young families with children. Children mean schools, and schools mean taxes. So Plymouth, the remnant of the "Old Colony" and thus the state's largest town (98 square miles), wallows in golf courses. As of 1998, six big courses were planned, one of twenty-seven holes. Residents see golfers, both those on private and those on municipal courses, as an asset. A golf course, as Plymouth's planner put it, is equivalent to 250 homes. Should we guess 500 children?[62]

Time-honored back-fence behavior also aggravates the effects of intertown competition for tax revenues. A stranger can reliably identify a town boundary by discovering where the town fathers have placed the dump or the sex shops. The town of Raynham has placed its zone for pornographic activities on the Bridgewater boundary.

Main Street Styles, Middleboro

Middleboro, forty-two miles south of Boston by highway, is a sort of lesser version of Framingham set in Plymouth County. Its population in 1990 was approximately 20,000. The residents had a low median household income, but not so low as that of suffering old mill towns and isolated rural places. There were a thousand people reported to be living below the federal poverty line, and small African American and Hispanic populations. Middleboro's immigrants came mostly from Cuba and the Dominican Republic.[63] Long a manufacturing town, it functioned for many years as an annex to Brockton's shoe industry. Its fame was threefold. Middleboro was the birthplace of P. T. Barnum's Mrs. Tom Thumb (née Lavinia Bump, 1841–1919). It was long the factory location of Maxim fire engines (from 1914 until the mill closed in 1987), and it serves as the headquarters of the Ocean Spray Cranberry producers' cooperative.[64] Middleboro's new fortune is arriving with a favorable intersection of I-495 and old U.S. Route 44 (Plymouth to Taunton to Providence). At this intersection developers are building a large industrial park to relieve the town's tax burden.

The town's property is being watched over by two very experienced and competent professionals, Jack Healey, the town manager, and Ruth Geoffroy, the town planner. The pair are arguing with state and federal highway engineers to limit the exits from the future Route 44 to two, so that the freeway's traffic will not pour down the town's old streets. They also have been very active in improving the town's environmental practices. Formerly Middleboro dumped raw sewage into brooks along the Nemasket River, a tributary of the region's large Taunton River. Now the town operates a secondary treatment plant and is tightening up its storm drains. Healy's halting of the overpumping of Assawompsett Pond is a unique intervention. New Bedford draws its water from this shallow lake, and sometimes in the summer that city pumped so intensely that it reversed the flow of the outlet river thereby trapping the herring in the pond. By jawboning and with state aid, a herring ladder has been rebuilt on the Nemasket River (Wareham Street), and local sportsmen volunteers supervise the annual herring run. This restoration of the herring has more than local significance. The herring are very important members of the Buzzards Bay environment.[65]

Elsewhere manager and planner face the common problems of their region. There are still a few dairy farms liable to be divided, and some of the cranberry bog owners' property may be cut up into patchwork residential plots. The attractive town center also requires constant attention. Healey brings to these tasks a very particular philosophy. He thinks that town plans and projects should grow out of a wide consensus. Such a practice requires many meetings and a readiness to compromise, but, he reminds a visitor, the results are always faster and better than a lawsuit. This philosophy has led him to join the Vision 2020 initiative and to plead for a new relationship between town and state. In common with all town officials, he wants the state to assume a much larger share of education expense. The school appropriation currently takes about 60 percent of any town's annual budget. He does not want fiscal competition to drive town development.

In addition, Healey wants new state and federal processes wherein local plans would become respected and incorporated into the planning process of the larger agencies. So far only the Massachusetts Executive Office of Environmental Affairs's Watershed Program has approached such a stance. In the state's river protection efforts it initiated a planning process that gathered all the drainage basin stakeholders in joint meetings. It is Healey's belief that if towns take the trouble to carefully work out their plans through the process of town meeting consensus, then such local goals and insights must be honored as knowledge of great integrity and therefore be worked into state and federal programs.[66]

So far the Vision 2020 group has proceeded cautiously. It began with the initiative of Mark Primack, the director of a small land trust, the Wildlands Trust of Southeastern Massachusetts (its office is in Duxbury). Primack, the former director of the Open Space Coalition in the city of Boston, foresaw that with the reopening of rail commuter lines to Plymouth and Middleboro fragmented development would likely rush in. He started talking about a regional organization. Next, Robert D. Yaro, the director of the New York Regional Plan Association, taught a studio class at the Harvard Graduate School of Design that focused on the Old Colony area. Yaro himself had formerly published studies advocating cluster development designs as a means of preserving the pastoral landscapes of western Massachusetts. He and his Harvard students published another such book, *A Region in Transition: The New Old Colony*, in 1996.

These initiatives brought together the area's three regional planning agencies, none of which possessed any governmental powers. These are the Southeastern Regional Planning and Economic Development District, the Old Colony Planning Council, and the Metropolitan Area Planning Council. In 1997 they pooled their resources to finance the establishment of a fifty-person task force whose job it was to begin a sustained organizing of the fifty-one cities and towns of Plymouth and Bristol counties. Donald Connors, a well-known environmental lawyer and planner and the author of the Cape Cod Commission legislation, was chosen to be chairman.

A year later the task force held a large meeting to seek approval for a set of regional goals. A carefully selected group of town officials, business leaders, active citizens, and environmental organization representatives lent political weight to the proceedings. Out of these October 1998 sessions came the commonsense goals that the 2020 group is now trying to attain. In briefest terms, the group wants to find ways to husband the region's natural resources and to coordinate its economic development with the preservation of its town centers and highly valued landscapes. The group also shares a deep concern for the provision of affordable housing and for some manner of fiscal relief to counteract current antichild town practices.[67]

To achieve these goals the 2020 group must invent some new institution or some new processes for intertown and town-state cooperation. The towns now see themselves as too numerous and too various to be willing to submit themselves to an overarching planning agency like the Cape Cod Commission. Connors notes that in the Cape case there was a general perception among the voters in all the towns during the late 1980s that development was out of control.[68] Such consensus is lacking in Plymouth and Bristol counties. Connors is a patient man. He expects that a sustained process of education and discussion will in time lead to some successful invention, perhaps the sort of cooperative behavior Jack Healey envisions. In 1999 the 2020 group began working with the Manomet Center for Environmental Sciences in Plymouth to conduct a full survey. Their task will be to pull together all the available information on the air, water, plants, fish, and wildlife of the fifty-one towns and to connect these data with information on land use and town circumstances. The hope of this initiative is to develop a regionwide portrait that can help each town to see just where it fits within the economy of the Boston city region, and within its special lowlands inheritance.[69]

More is at issue in this project than private property, fresh water, and fish. The 2020 group is trying to find some process whereby citizens now organized in separate towns, citizens of towns that are often managed by volunteers, can strike some balance between the dictates of local values and traditions and the exigencies of an urban regional existence. Don Connors says, wisely enough, "You cannot change these towns."[70] But these towns will change. Boston's towns have been self-governing entities of some sort since 1620, and in the ensuing years they have continually reinvented themselves. Some have chosen to become municipalities with mayors and councils, some have adopted representative town meetings, others have adapted the old forms by mixing professional managers with volunteer boards. It now remains to be discovered if the inescapable development demands and their accompanying intertown impacts can find appropriate forms and practices.

AN OVERVIEW

At this moment in the transformation of the settlement patterns of the Boston region everyone would welcome a reliable prediction of what might be looked for next. Two obstacles stand in the path of such an undertaking. First, the variety among the 204 cities and towns does not lend itself to an easy summary. Second, evaluation is further obscured by the vagueness of the current debating term *sprawl*. Sprawl is a hostile image that lacks any suggestions to direct someone's attention to the processes of change that have been, or are, at work. It certainly does not entertain the idea of unexpected outcomes. Yet, the consequences of the building that has gone on since 1950 are freighted with unexpected outcomes.

For example, in 1950 Americans feared the possible return of economic depression and severe unemployment. The term *development* was then a term of hope that promised new construction, jobs, something fresh, prosperity, and progress. In Boston, with its continuing local depression, development was especially prized. Now

Main Street, Town Green, Tewksbury

Main Street, Utilities, Tewksbury

developer and development can be used as swear words. In cities that experienced the clearances for highways and urban renewal these terms evoke memories of past injustices. In distant towns the new retail strips, malls, and tracts of houses and condominium villages often destroy the special look and special character of a place. Tewksbury in 1950 was getting by as a small farm town of carnation growers, summer cottages, and a state hospital. Now it is home to highway interchanges, malls, and industrial parks. These newcomers have kept the taxes low for the owners of the many new houses, but Tewksbury today is indistinguishable from a thousand other places in the United States. Did Tewksbury residents expect such an outcome? It seems unlikely.

Such events are forcing many Boston towns to initiate a long process of meetings to discover whether the town's residents can agree on what elements are commonly valued and therefore worth preserving. Prof. Richard T. T. Forman of Harvard's Department of Landscape Architecture, and a resident of Concord, has devised a procedure for the simultaneous evaluation of the environmental and historical resources of a town so that public discussion of the two

Main Street, from the parking lot, Tewksbury

could go forward simultaneously. For any community unhappy about
the uniformities of current land development, this method holds
great promise. Boston also possesses a special advantage in such
a process. The sizes of its municipalities and townships are small,
so that a citizen's everyday experiences usually provide sufficient
knowledge for an intelligent debate.

The automobile itself has proven itself a hornet's nest of surprises. In 1950 it was regarded as the hallmark of personal freedom, and the two-car family, one for the husband and one for the
wife, stood as a universal ideal. Traffic, to be sure, was stop-and-go
everywhere, but the planned freeways gave promise that the private car could realize its potential. Now, daily freeway traffic jams
mock those expectations. Boston has the good fortune to possess
a considerable transit and rail system, but public transportation is
used only for about 10 percent of the region's trips. Some inner suburbs and towns along commuter rail lines are especially favored,
but crossregion movement is everywhere a problem. Here again the
Boston inheritance of town centers and a network of old cities suggests a ready solution for additional public transportation. So far,

however, public transportation is viewed politically as a taxpayer expense rather than as a way that families might reduce their travel budgets by pooling their tax resources. At present no bus line offers patrons at each and every stop a neat, clean shelter from the rain and snow. Surely such neglect tells of a culture of low public regard for travelers without a private car.

In the 1950s a distinguished Harvard law professor and a corporate lawyer wrote an article about the underutilization of the region's rivers.[71] At that time they commonly served as public sewers. Water abounded, and no one objected to the wasteful practices that then destroyed much of its quality. Now, water usage has gone up, new settlements demand service from small town systems, and there are water shortages throughout the region. The Boston region's town-by-town structure hampers remedial action, since water, fresh and waste water both, must be managed as it flows, watershed by watershed. Active citizens and the U.S. Environmental Protection Agency have much improved the Charles River, but fragmented management hampers remedial action throughout the region.

The poverty rates of the region have also not remained constant. In 1950 parts of the Boston region appeared regularly on federal distress lists. Now the new diversified economy seems more secure — not immune from recessions, like the computer manufacturing collapse of the 1980s, but safer. Changes in federal policy have also shifted the incidence of poverty. During the 1950s the elderly dominated the lists of the impoverished. Now, thanks to Social Security and health legislation, they no longer do so. Their place has been taken by women and children and new migrants.

The latest federal welfare reform requires all able-bodied adults to work, and it places the responsibility on the Commonwealth of Massachusetts to carry out that mandate. The state, in turn, has launched a variety of programs for wage supplements, for day care, for transportation, for on-the-job training, and the like, all of which are parceled out to municipal, private, and charitable groups through a system of grants. Federal and state administrators have fostered this nest of decentralized activities in the hope that on-the-spot, local knowledge and action is likely to be most effective. In its dispersal this latest welfare program resembles the long-standing town-by-town charity of old. It remains to be seen if such a structure will succeed within today's climate of rapidly changing employment opportunities. The continued presence of a large and politically invisible native and immigrant poor population living beyond the gaze of the region's centralized media stands in mute warning against optimism.

Here in the Boston region, as throughout the United States, full employment and prosperity have brought further surprises. Many families now require two wage earners in order to pay for housing and transportation. Overtime and additional small jobs provide the extras. Among the well-to-do the two-income household also prevails, and because of the hours demanded of management, marketing, and professional employees, here too the shortage of free time prevails. Thus, ever more cars and ever faster means of communication have combined to rob their possessors of discretionary time. It is a lesson that Thoreau preached long ago, but few among us heeded his warnings. Today our teachers complain of parents who lack time to parent their children. Those concerned to maintain local communities with informal volunteer organizations give dire predictions. Physicians who treat the symptoms of stress bewail both the loss of free time and many of the popular ways in which we spend what we have. Although ours is now an incredibly prosperous society compared to 1950, many now often place the word *consumer* next to the word *developer* on our list of pejoratives.

In this situation it is possible to imagine two alternative futures for the Boston region. The first carries recent trends into the future. Accordingly, the regional dispersal would continue; open land would be taken up with ever more houses being set apart on large lots, as local zoning laws now require. Developers would continue to seek busy roads and highway intersections for new office, industrial, and retail clusters, thereby continuing the weakening of former town centers. Only wealthy towns with a strong preservation and conservation tradition would be likely to mitigate these trends. The costs of transportation, municipal services, and housing would continue to rise in order to serve dispersed settlements of high energy consumption, heavy waste production, and needs for extensive infrastructure and service provision.

In such a future much of what makes the Boston region valuable would be lost to the repetition of uniformities. This is preeminently a place of small things: occasional clusters of buildings, little landscape passages, the continuation of local institutions. Such particularities distinguish Boston places from elsewhere. Today many small elements still survive. The recent habits of large uniform roads, highways, subdivisions, strip malls, and corporate marketing, however, inevitably destroy such particularity, as might the gentlest and kindest tread of the elephant's foot were it set down in the wrong place.

Since many of us would like to imagine an alternative to such a future, it would be well to realize that the physical and geographical revolution that was wrought during the past fifty years was propelled by a popular consensus for the good life whose momentum reached its apogee during the 1950s and has been declining since. The elements that built that momentum consisted of a set of decisions that every generation must make for itself: the nature of the family, the ways of child rearing, the terms of employment, the modes of transportation, and the provision of housing. Only the condition of the natural environment of the region lacked attention during these years. Such a list of elements immediately suggests that had the public chosen differently the Boston region today would look quite otherwise than it does. A quick review of that past can suggest the possibilities for an alternative future.

The cultural consensus of the 1950s surged forward as a welcome healing wave. The nation had just experienced two decades of severe economic depression and the carnage and dislocations of war. We all hoped that the family might offer a source for restoration. Young couples married, had children, and left the old cities and towns for new houses and yards in the suburbs. There they hoped children could safely play, new schools and churches would support the newcomers, and good wages and hours would pay for the car and the mortgage. At the core of this cultural consensus, giving it its energy, stood the young mother and the automobile. The mother would read books about child care and talk to her contemporaries and resolve to do better than her mother had. The automobile, in turn, connected her to her parental networks and to the newly developing suburban ways.

At the same time, the Boston region enjoyed the presence of a number of talented architects, a few of whom turned their attention to domestic architecture. The Architects Collaborative (TAC), whose stars were Walter Gropius (1883–1969) and Benjamin Thompson (1918–), and the independent Carl Koch (1912–98) can be singled out as providing examples of the best work. TAC designed and built two subdivisions, Six Moon Hill (Lexington, 1950) and Five Fields (Lexington, 1952). Koch built Snake Hill (Belmont, 1945) and Conantum (Concord, 1957) and a very successful manufactured house.[72] The special quality of this work lay in its simplicity of means and its careful attention to domestic life. By today's inflated standards, these houses were tiny and their materials modest. The designs fused the style elements of Frank Lloyd Wright, California and New England houses, and Scandinavian precedents. Careful attention was given to the design of the kitchen, to the layout of open room plans to make small spaces function as larger ones, to connecting the interior of the house visually and practically to the outside surroundings, and to the arrangement of the houses on their lots so that there might be both privacy and the sense of community.

The ordinary home buyer could not afford this custom work, but the small Capes and ramblers that sprang up everywhere had glass doors to connect to decks and yards and open plans with family rooms extending from a modern workspace kitchen. Community-held open space and community pools and clubs were rare in the 1950s, but the presence of many young families, all with children, turned a cookie-cutter street into an instant community. Later, the shared open land and the closed circuit of streets of TAC's and Koch's examples became the clichés of cul-de-sacs and expensive subdivisions. At this time neither the best design, nor the worst, would meet today's environmental goals because the site was not considered in its relationship to the larger environment in which it took its place. The best houses of this era do, however, suggest how we might recapture a more suitable future than what is now being constructed.

Since the 1950s all the elements of that domestic consensus have changed. Stay-at-home wives and mothers are now a minority among mothers with children; the family itself is experimenting with a variety of forms from gay and lesbian households to men and women who just live together. An ever-increasing proportion of households consists of single individuals. Except for new immigrants to the region, parents are raising fewer children, and as a consequence there are whole blocks, even subdivisions, without children. For its part, the automobile has multiplied and so also have the number of trips it makes, but it is now just a well-upholstered piece of work, no longer a key to personal freedom. Finally, the small starter houses of the 1950s have disappeared from the new house market. Many towns zone against them for fear that they might harbor young families with children. Also, home builders find little profit in small units. The builders' situation is improved by the popular "mansion" styles, which are three times the size of the 1950s homes.

It is not difficult to imagine that under these new circumstances the region's future could better accommodate itself by taking advantage of recent tendencies. The preservation movement has been strong here, where old buildings, picturesque streets, and villages attract tourists and also give satisfaction to their residents. The historic neighborhoods of the city of Boston itself have, once again, become the homes of the rich and the fashionable. The environmental movement has a strong following from people concerned with the preservation of birds, regulating hunting and fishing, and protecting the resources of rivers and estuaries. Should the architectural preservationists and the environmentalists find ways to make common cause, as they have in Concord, towns could easily find the means to put new development in its proper locations.

If the preservationists and the environmentalists might team up with those concerned with affordable housing, a positive new politics could come to the fore. Because the Boston region is just now prosperous and popular, and because the region's land is cut up into small parcels, housing here is very expensive. Zoning for acre and half-acre lots is now the most common rule, and it prevents matching wants and needs to places. Already some cities and towns have relaxed their regulations to encourage infill housing and apartments near existing centers. It is likely that this reform will continue to grow in popularity. What is missing is a fiscal adjustment by the state so that towns are no longer rewarded for excluding children.

In the end the revival of a city- and town-centered mode of building and rebuilding requires a general appreciation of the high family costs of the two- and three-car household. There are many possible avenues for relief, which range from special commuter minibus services to full-scale bus and rail transit. At the moment in the spread-out Boston region, household time and money budgets await imaginative and multiple responses for linking up the outer centers.

Such an alternative future for the region is possible, some of it probable. Water shortages, traffic delays, strip malls, housing shortages, and impoverished old mill towns militate against continuing as in the past. Many towns are experimenting with denser developments than those of the recent past, and the cities are encouraging infill housing as part of their affordable housing programs. A hard question, however, hangs over from the past. For the past century the wealthy towns with historical and natural amenities have been able to preserve and even improve their special advantages. The ordinary workaday cities and towns have lacked both the resources and the politics necessary to do so. It remains to be seen if such cities and towns will now respond to the new possibilities of family, community, and environmental goals that will enable them to preserve their inheritance and to build afresh.

We all know what the Boston region will look like if it continues to expand along the paths of the previous half century. It will come more and more to resemble every other area of the United States, except that it will have a seashore and a lot of trees. Should, however, a local and state politics of preservation, care for families and children, and environmentalism emerge, then it is possible to imagine a region peppered with active village and town centers and reworked old mill towns that are newly linked by varieties of public transportation. The look of the region would be quite new because its green lands and open spaces would not resemble the parks and greenbelts of past urban inventions but would be something quite new—a linking of the open lands and river edges from city to town to town in a continuous reticulation of large and small areas whose shapes would mimic the inherited Boston land forms themselves. In such a pattern the special natural assets of each city and town would be joined to form a regional bank of natural resources and public recreation.

N O T E S

Introduction

1. Edwin O'Connor (1918–1968), *The Edge of Sadness* (Boston: Little Brown, 1961).

2. John Kerouac (1922–1957), *On the Road* (New York: Viking Press, 1957).

3. Robert Lowell (1917–1977), *Life Studies, and For the Union Dead* (New York: Farrar, Straus & Giroux, 1964).

4. John Gunther, *Inside USA* (New York: Harper & Brothers, 1947).

5. A majority in the town of Weston found the idea of strangers pedaling down a bicycle pathway unacceptable (*Boston Globe, West*, Dec. 7, 1997, *Boston Globe*, Feb. 4, 1998); a vociferous group in Hingham thought the restoration of a commuter rail line would endanger their town (*Boston Globe*, March 5, July 1, 1999.)

Chapter 1. Geography

1. John O'Keefe and David R. Foster, "An Ecological History of Massachusetts Forests," *Arnoldia* 58 (summer 1998): 2–31.

2. U.S. Department of Transportation, Bureau of the Census, *Census Transportation Planning Package: 1990*, computer disk set (Washington, D.C.: Government Printing Office, 1990); Sam Bass Warner, Jr., *The Way We Really Live* (Boston: Boston Public Library, 1977), 1–9.

3. Tom Wessels, *Reading the Forested Landcape: A Natural History of New England* (Woodstock, Vt.: Countryman Press, 1997).

4. Despite the absence of petroleum under New England's ground, it is an intensely studied area, subject to continuing geological research whose conclusions are rapidly changing our understanding of the past. I would like to thank Lindy

Elkins of MIT, Meg Thompson of Wellesley College, and William A. Newman of Northeastern University for their help in explaining this history to me.

5. Margaret D. Thompson et al., "Tectonostratigraphic Implications of Late Pro-
   terozoic U-Pb Zircon Ages in the Avalon Zone of Southeastern New England,"
   in Margaret D. Thompson and R. Damian Nance, eds., *Avalonian and Related
   Peri-Gondwanan Terranes of the Circum-North Atlantic*, Special Paper no. 304
   (Boulder, Colo.: Geological Society of America, 1996), 179–91.

6. Robert N. Oldale, *Geologic History of Cape Cod, Massachusetts* (Washington,
   D.C.: U.S. Department of the Interior, Geologic Survey, 1981), 8.

7. David Woodhouse et al., "Geology of Boston, Massachusetts, United States of
   America," *Bulletin of the Association of Engineering Geologists* 28 (November
   1991): 386/2, 389/2, 399 (fig. 14 shows the river's path), 400/2.

8. John Winthrop, "An Account of the Earthquake Felt in New England, and Neighboring Parts of America on the 18th of November, 1755," *Philosophical Transactions
   of the Royal Society* 50, pt. 1 (1755): 11.

9. John E. Ebel, "The Seventeenth-Century Seismicity of Northeastern North
   America," *Seismological Research Letters* 67 (May–June 1996): 51–68; John E.
   Ebel and Alan L. Kafka, "Earthquake Activity in the Northeastern United States,"
   in D. Burton Slemmons et al., eds., *Neotectonics of North America* (Boulder, Colo.:
   Geological Society of America, 1991), 277–90; *Boston Globe*, Jan. 11, 1999.

10. Woodhouse, "Geology of Boston," 401/2.

11. Clifford A. Kaye, *The Geology and Early History of the Boston Area of Massachu-
    setts*, Geological Survey Bulletin 1476 (Washington, D.C.: Government Printing
    Office, 1976), 6; Woodhouse, "Geology of Boston," 401/2.

12. Kingsbury Pond is now a subject of conflict, drawn down by Franklin Well no. 4.
    Oldale, *Geologic History of Cape Cod*.

13. Neil Jorgensen, *Southern New England* (San Francisco: Sierra Club Books, 1978),
    88–91, 97.

14. Jorgensen, *Southern New England*, 112–13, 206; Charles H. W. Foster, ed., *Step-
    ping Back to Look Forward: A History of the Massachusetts Forest* (Cambridge:
    Harvard University Press, 1998).

15. Michael Berrill and Deborah Berrill, *The North Atlantic Coast* (San Francisco:
    Sierra Club Books, 1981), 29–31.

16. Gordon Abbott, Jr., *Saving Special Places: A Centennial History of the Trustees of Reservations* (Ipswich, Mass.: Ipswich Press, 1993).

17. Carl Seaburg, Alan Seaburg, and Thomas Dahill, *The Incredible Ditch: A Bicentennial History of the Middlesex Canal* (Medford, Mass.: Medford Historical Society, 1997); Burt VerPlanck, *Middlesex Canal Guide and Maps* (Billerica, Mass.: Middlesex Canal Association, 1998).

18. F. J. Wood, "The Toll Road—Our First Public Utility," *Public Service Journal* 20 (February 1917): 93–102; Oscar Handlin and Mary Flug Handlin, *Commonwealth: A Study of the Role of Government in the American Economy: Massachusetts, 1774–1861* (1947; reprint, Cambridge: Harvard University Press, 1969), 111–12; Map, "State of Massachusetts," from Mathew Carey, *American Atlas* (1804), Harvard Map Collection.

19. Theodore Steinberg, *Nature Incorporated: Industrialization and the Waters of New England* (New York: Cambridge University Press, 1991).

20. A Williams Company, "Railroad and Township Map of Massachusetts" (Boston: Boston Map Store, 1882), Harvard Map Collection.

21. Warner, *The Way We Really Live*, 43.

Chapter 2. How We Make Our Living

1. *Boston Globe*, May 20, 1998, H-10.

2. Keane Inc., 1995 and 1997 Annual Reports to Shareholders; *Boston Globe*, May 20, 1998, H-6, 25.

3. *Boston Globe*, May 20, 1998, H-8, 24.

4. *Boston Globe*, May 20, 1998, H-9.

5. Massachusetts Technology Collaborative, *Index of the Massachusetts Innovation Economy: 1997* (Westborough, Mass.: 1997), 7.

6. Interview, James D. Worden, Oct. 15, 1998; *New York Times*, Mar. 6, 1994.

7. *Massachusetts Innovative Economy: 1997*, 7.

8. *Massachusetts Innovative Economy: 1997*, 9.

9. *Wall Street Journal*, Dec. 28, 1995; *Boston Globe*, May 20, 1998, H-15; *New York Times*, Nov. 4, 1998.

10. Interview, John Abele, Nov. 12, 1997.

11. Mrs. Sarah S. B. Yule of the First Unitarian Church of Oakland contributed the

phrase to an anthology published by the Ladies of the Church in February 1912. Reprinted in Bruce Bohle, *Home Book of American Quotations* (New York: Dodd, Mead, 1967), 151.

12. Parametric Corporation, Annual Reports, 1996 and 1997; interview, John D. Stuart, vice president for corporate marketing, Nov. 24, 1997.

13. *Boston Globe*, May 20, 1998, H-6, 27.

14. *Boston Globe*, Aug. 28, 1998.

15. *Boston Business Journal*, Mar. 8–14, 1996, 3.

16. Hologic, *Annual Report, 1996*; *Boston Globe*, May 20, 1997, C-8; interview, Jay Stein, Nov. 19, 1997.

17. Stein interview, Nov. 19, 1997; Annalee Saxenian, *Regional Advantage, Culture, and Cooperation in Silicon Valley and Route 128* (Cambridge: Harvard University Press, 1994).

18. Jonathan D. Sarna and Ellen Smith, eds., *The Jews of Boston* (Boston: Combined Jewish Philanthropies of Greater Boston, 1995).

19. *Harvard v. Amory*, 9 Pick. 461 (1830).

20. Wallace Stegner and the editors of *Look*, *One Nation* (Boston: Houghton Mifflin, 1945).

21. Interview, Lawrence J. Lasser, Oct. 22, 1998.

22. Lasser interview, Oct. 22, 1998.

23. *Putnam Investments* (1998).

24. Interview, Charles "Mike" Daley, CEO, LoJack Corporation, May 21, 1998.

25. Ian Ayres and Steven D. Levitt, "Measuring Positive Externalities from Unobservable Victim Protection: An Empirical Analysis of LoJack," *Quarterly Journal of Economics* (February 1998): 43–77.

26. Interview, Alan Symonds, Oct. 5, 1998.

27. *New York Times*, Jan. 27, 1991.

28. Interview, Cynthia Gordon, May 19, 1998.

29. *Boston Globe*, Aug. 27, 1998.

30. Interview, Angel Martinez, Oct. 7, 1998.

31. Martinez interview, Oct. 7, 1998.

32. *New York Times*, Oct. 14, 1995.

33. *New York Times*, Nov. 5, 1998.

34. *Footwear News*, Nov. 10, 1997, 12.

Chapter 3. So You Want to Be a Yankee?

1. William Bradford, *Of Plymouth Plantation, 1620–1647*, ed. Samuel Eliot Morison (New York: Knopf, 1970), 253, 334.

2. Sam Bass Warner, Jr., *The Province of Reason* (Cambridge: Harvard University Press, 1984), 44; Cleveland Amory, *The Proper Bostonians* (New York: Dutton, 1947).

3. Interview, Buzzy Bartone, Sept. 22, 1997.

4. Interview, Carol Pimentel, Nov. 21, 1997.

5. Interview, Roger Woods, Oct. 6, 1997.

6. Interview, Mary Allor, Oct. 29, 1997.

7. Interview, Larry Walsh, Sept. 19, 1997.

8. *Boston Globe*, Jan. 8, 1997. Ms. Scott's neighborhood is the gang-ridden "four corners," Washington and Bowdoin Streets, Dorchester.

9. Interview, Edward O'Brien, Feb. 5, 1998.

10. *Boston Globe*, Dec. 14, 1996.

11. Interview, Karin Gertsch, Sept. 26, 1997.

12. *Boston Globe*, June 27, 1998.

13. Interview, Lynda Simkins, Oct. 7, 1997.

14. Interview, Elizabeth Berg, Sept. 10, 1997; *Boston Globe*, May 15, 1997.

15. *Boston Globe, South*, Apr. 6, 1997.

16. *Boston Globe, South*, Mar. 22, 1998.

17. *Boston Globe*, Feb. 15, 1998.

18. *Boston Globe*, Billerica, Apr. 19, 1999; Salem, Apr. 19, 1999 Salisbury, Apr. 20, 1999; Kingston, June 10, 1999.

19. *Boston Globe, South*, Nov. 23, 1997; *Boston Globe*, May 19, 1999.

20. *Boston Globe, West*, Apr. 13, 1997.

21. Interview, William McDevitt, Nov. 23, 1997.

22. Edith Horner, ed., *Massachusetts Municipal Profiles, 1998–1999* (Palo Alto, Calif.: Information Publications, 1998).

23. Interview, Michael Arrato Gavrish, Oct. 18, 1998.

24. *Boston Globe*, May 24, 1998.

25. *Boston Globe*, May 26, 1998.

26. Data sources: Wayne Moody, ed., *Patterson's Elementary Education, 1999 Edition*, vol. 11 (Mount Prospect, Ill.: Educational Directories, 1999); Horner, *Massachusetts Municipal Profiles, 1998–1999*.

27. Deirdre A. Gaquin and Mark Littman, *1999 County and City Extra* (Washington, D.C.: Bernan Press, 1999), table B, cols. 133–35.

28. Robin Dunbar, *Grooming, Gossip, and the Evolution of Language* (Cambridge: Harvard University Press, 1996), 69–79. Theodore Sizer, in his *Horace's Compromise: The Dilemma of the American High School* (Boston: Houghton Mifflin, 1982), 254, n. 12, has reviewed the literature of school size and function and concludes that it is not a significant variable in respect to student performance. Instead, he notes that teacher quality is most important. In his latest book, written with his wife, Nancy Faust Sizer, he has become a keen advocate for small schools. *The Students Are Watching* (Boston: Beacon Press, 1999).

29. Interview, Frank Gersony, June 18, 1999.

30. Ms. McGinty's essay sent to the author by Ms. Nivica, along with other essays on the same topic. Interview, Lynne Nivica, May 1, 1999.

31. Interview, Suzanne Belanger, June 14, 1999.

32. Interview, George Cheevers, Feb. 20, 1999.

33. Interview, Abe Abadi, Feb. 27, 1999.

34. Interview, Joan Vodoklys, May 19, 1999.

35. Interview, John Conaty, June 20, 1999.

36. Sizer, *Horace's Compromise*, 38; Deborah Meier, *The Power of Their Ideas* (Boston: Beacon Press, 1995), 10.

37. *Minneapolis Star-Tribune*, Apr. 4, 1999.

38. Interview, Rev. Alfred J. Hicks, S.J., Apr. 24, 1999.

39. Nativity Prep visit, Apr. 30, 1999.

40. *Mission Hill School News*, 2, May 15, May 24, 1999.

41. *Boston Globe*, Jan. 13, 1999.

42. *Boston Globe*, Jan. 13, 1999; Meier, *Power of Their Ideas*, 24–26, 107–19.

43. *Mission Hill School News*, 2, Jan. 19, 1999; Deborah Meier, *Will Standards Save Public Education?* (Boston: Beacon Press, 2000).

44. *Mission Hill School News*, 2, June 1, 1999.

Chapter 4. Making Music

1. Interview, Milo Miles, Aug. 24, 1998.

2. Evan Eisenberg, *The Recording Angel: Explorations in Phonography* (New York: McGraw-Hill, 1987), 25–32.

3. Interview, Jack Coffey III, Coffee Music Co., Norwood, Mass., July 15, 1998; Robert Cutietta, Donald L. Hamann, and Linda Miller Walker, "The Extra-Musical Advantages of a Musical Education," *Spin-Offs* (Elkhart, Ind.: United Musical Instruments, 1995).

4. "1997–1998 Directory," *Symphony* 48 (January 1997). A 1997 survey titled "Public Participation in the Arts," for the National Endowment for the Arts, revealed that among adults eighteen years and older, 24.3 percent of Massachusetts informants reported attending at least one classical music concert during the year, versus 15.6 percent nationally. Also, Mark Schuster of MIT, using this same survey, constructed a composite participation in the arts variable that included singing and playing a musical instrument as well as dance and theater. Here Massachusetts adults (45 percent) were second only to Florida residents (47.6 percent) and well above the U.S. average of 40.8 percent. Survey by Westat, Rockville, Md., SPPA CD-ROM.

5. Harriet Beecher Stowe in her novel about Natick circa 1800, *Oldtown Folks*, makes fun of "our country psalmody" (1869; reprint, New Brunswick, N.J.: Rutgers University Press, 1987), 56.

6. H. Wiley Hitchcock, *Music in the United States: A Historical Introduction*, 3d ed. (Englewood Cliffs, N.J.: Prentice-Hall, 1988), 5–10.

7. Hitchcock, *Music in the United States*, 20.

8. Hitchcock, *Music in the United States*, 66–67, 81–84.

9. Andrea Olmstead, "A History of the Boston Conservatory of Music" (Boston Conservatory of Music, June 1985, manuscript).

10. Bruce McPherson and James Klein, *Measure by Measure: A History of the*

New England Conservatory from 1867 (Boston: New England Conservatory, 1995), 35.

11. Hitchcock, *Music in the United States*, 111–12.

12. Barbara Owen, *The Organ in New England: An Account of Its Use and Manufacture to the End of the Nineteenth Century* (Randolph, Mass.: Sunbury Press, 1979).

13. Mark Anthony DeWolfe Howe, *The Boston Symphony Orchestra, 1881–1931*, semicentennial ed. (Boston: Houghton Mifflin, 1931), 13, 17.

14. McPherson and Klein, *Measure by Measure*, 28.

15. McPherson and Klein, *Measure by Measure*, 63–64, 73, 90–91.

16. Hitchcock, *Music in the United States*, 145.

17. Interview, Robert Freeman, Sept. 15, 1998.

18. McPherson and Klein, *Measure by Measure*, 70, 75.

19. Jean McBee Knox, *The Longy School of Music: The First 75 Years* (Watertown, Mass.: Windflower Press, 1991), 9–11, 14.

20. Knox, *Longy School*, 29–39.

21. Knox, *Longy School*, 61–65.

22. Interview, Victor Rosenbaum, Dec. 2, 1998.

23. Ed Hazell, *Berklee: The First Fifty Years* (Boston: Berklee Press, 1995), 4, 7–8.

24. Hazell, *Berklee*, 10.

25. Hazell, *Berklee*, 12–13.

26. Hazell, *Berklee*, 29.

27. Hazell, *Berklee*, 29, 44.

28. Hazell, *Berklee*, 42, 73, 109.

29. Hazell, *Berklee*, 48, 288.

30. Eric Von Schmidt and Jim Rooney, *Baby, Let Me Follow You Down: The Illustrated Story of the Cambridge Folk Years* (Amherst: University of Massachusetts Press, 1979).

31. Hazell, *Berklee*, 103.

32. Hazell, *Berklee*, 77–79, 111, 119, 132.

33. McPherson and Klein, *Measure by Measure*, 131–33.

34. Hazell, *Berklee*, 170, 183; Berklee College of Music, *1998-1999 Bulletin*, 68.

35. Hazell, *Berklee*, 208.

36. Interview, David Hoose, Dec. 1, 1998.

37. Interview, Herb Pomeroy, Nov. 6, 1998.

38. Interview, Nicholas Kitchen, Jan. 11, 1999.

39. Interview, Shizue Sano, Dec. 9, 1998.

40. Interview, Ann Marie Lindquist, founder of the Greater Boston Choral Consortium, Dec. 14, 1998; *Boston Globe Calendar*, Nov. 21, 1996.

41. Interview, William E. Thomas, Nov. 10, 1998.

42. Harry Haskell, *The Early Music Revival: A History* (New York: Thames & Hudson, 1988), 105–9; Larry Palmer, *The Harpsichord in America: A Twentieth Century Revival* (Bloomington: Indiana University Press, 1989).

43. Palmer, *Harpsichord*, 117.

44. Joel Cohen and Herb Snitzer, *Reprise: The Extraordinary Revival of Early Music* (Boston: Little, Brown, 1985), 88.

45. Interview, Laura and Daniel Stepner, Jan. 6, 1999.

46. Robert H. Frank and Philip J. Cook, *The Winner Take All Society* (New York: Free Press, 1995).

47. *Boston Globe*, Apr. 18, 1999.

48. Interview, Brad Paul, Rounder Records, Sept. 21, 1998; Andrew Goldman, "Outlawed," *Boston Magazine* 90 (August 1998): 132–83.

49. Wendy M. Grossman, "Putting the Squeeze on Music," *Scientific American* 280 (May 1999): 38–39.

50. I am indebted to Milo Miles, music editor of Soundstone, interviewed Aug. 24, 1998, and Herb Pomeroy, interviewed Nov. 1, 1998, for my understanding of a popular singer's or band's situation.

51. Paul Broadnax, interview, Sept. 18, 1998.

52. Laurie Geltman, interviews, Sept. 10, 1998, Oct. 7, 1998, June 3, 1999.

53. Bill Morrissey, interviews, Dec. 14, 1998, Jan. 6, 1999.

54. Bill Morrissey, "Different Currency," *You'll Never Get to Heaven*, CD, Rounder Records, 1996.

55. Ellen Pfeiffer, *Boston Herald*, June 4, 1998; Daniel Pinkham, interview, Jan. 19, 1999.

56. Roy Urwin, "Many Scores and Organs Galore," *Clavier* (April 1999): 14.

57. Scott Wheeler, interview, Jan. 13, 1999.

58. Charles E. Ives, *Memos*, ed. John Kirkpatrick (New York: Norton, 1972), 132.

Chapter 5. Changing Places

1. Alice J. Rarig, Projection, *Population of Massachusetts Cities and Towns, Year 2000 and 2010* (Amherst: Massachusetts Institute for Social and Economic Research, December 1994), A 3-1.

2. Interview, David Soule and Jean Christensen, Metropolitan Area Planning Council, Oct. 13, 1999.

3. Charles A. Maguire and Associates and the Joint Board for the Metropolitan Master Highway Plan, *The Master Plan for the Boston Metropolitan Area* (Boston: Commonwealth of Massachusetts, February 1, 1948).

4. George Sandborn, "Reference Notebook," typescript, State Transportation Library, Boston.

5. Alan Lupo, Frank Colcord, and Edmund P. Fowler, *Rites of Way: The Politics of Transportation in Boston and the U.S. City* (Boston: Little, Brown, 1971).

6. Stephen Falbel, *The Demographics of Commuting in Greater Boston*, 2d ed., rev. (Boston: Central Transportation Planning Staff, August 1998), fig. 4.

7. Cynthia Zaitzevsky, *Frederick Law Olmsted and the Boston Park System* (Cambridge: Harvard University Press, 1982), 33–46, 127–32; Sylvester Baxter, *Boston Park Guide* (Boston, 1889).

8. *Master Plan for the Boston Metropolitan Area*, 8.

9. Charles Eliot, Sr., *Charles Eliot, Landscape Architect* (Boston, 1902), 308, 312–18; Keith N. Morgan, "Charles Eliot, Landscape Architect: An Introduction to His Life and Work," *Arnoldia* (summer 1999): 2–21.

10. *Report of the Commission on Rapid Transit* (Boston: Commonwealth of Massachusetts, April 2, 1945), 10, 93.

11. Massachusetts Division of Metropolitan Planning, *Annual Report for the Year . . . 1925*, Public Document no. 54 (Boston, Commonwealth of Massachusetts, 1926), 11–13; Robert Whitten, *Report on a Thoroughfare Plan for Boston* (Boston: City of Boston, 1930), 11.

12. Massachusetts Department of Public Works, Division of Highways, "Route Map of Massachusetts, 1925," Massachusetts State Archives; Massachusetts Department of Public Works, *Annual Report . . . 1926*, Public Document no. 54 (Boston: Commonwealth of Massachusetts, 1927).

13. Massachusetts Division of Metropolitan Planning, *Annual Report . . . 1930*, Public Document no. 142 (Boston: Commonwealth of Massachusetts, 1931), 2–3.

14. G. H. Delano, "Memoir of Franklin Calhoun Pillsbury," *Transactions of the American Society of Civil Engineers* 103 (1938): 1861–63.

15. Donald Levitan, "Highway Development and Local Government: An Analysis of Relationships—A Case Study of Massachusetts Route 128" (Ph.D. diss., New York University, 1972), 49, 66–67.

16. Charles S. Bird, Jr., *Report of the Governor's Committee on the Needs and Uses of Open Spaces* (Boston: Commonwealth of Massachusetts, 1929), 6 and map.

17. Trustees of the Public Reservations, *Bay Circuit* (Boston: Trustees, 1937); Benton MacKaye, "Highway Approaches to Boston, A Wayside Situation and What to Do about It," *Bulletin no. 2*, (Boston: Trustees of the Public Reservations, 1931).

18. *Boston Globe*, *West*, Sept. 21, 1997; *Boston Globe*, *North*, Apr. 26, 1998.

19. Falbel, *Demographics of Commuting*, figs. 17–22.

20. Levitan, "Highway Development," 44–54, 76.

21. Interview, John Leary, chief counsel, Massachusetts Department of Transportation, Sept. 30, 1999; George Sandborn, "Reference Notebook," Massachusetts State Transportation Library; Falbel, *Demographics of Commuting*, fig. 4.

22. Charles E. Goodhue, Jr., *Ipswich: Proud Settlement in the Province of Massachusetts-Bay* (New York: Newcomen Society, 1953), 21–29.

23. Interview, Glenn G. Gibbs, director, Department of Planning and Development, Town of Ipswich, Nov. 8, 1999.

24. Statistics from Metropolitan Area Planning Council, *MAPC Community Profiles, 1998* (Boston: MAPC, 1998); U.S. Bureau of the Census, *1990 Census of Population, Social and Economic Characteristics, Massachusetts*, sec. 1 (Washington, D.C.: Government Printing Office, September 1993), table 3.

25. Carroll L. Cabot, *The Great House* (Beverly, Mass.: Trustee of Public Reservations, 1992).

26. Interview, Glenn G. Gibbs, Nov. 8, 1999.

27. Interview, Carolyn Britt, planner and member Ipswich Growth Management Committee, Oct. 15, 1999.

28. Kerry Mackin and Lou Wagner, *Ipswich River Basin Conservation Report Card* (Ips-

wich: Ipswich River Watershed Association and Massachusetts Audubon Society, 1999), 6.

29. Charles M. Haar and Barbara Gordon, "Riparian Water Rights vs. a Prior Appropriation System: A Comparison," *Boston University Law Review* 38 (1958): 207–55.

30. Interviews, Kerry Mackin, Oct. 3, 1997, Oct. 15, 1999.

31. *Boston Globe*, Nov. 29, 1997; *Metro West Daily News*, Nov. 15, 1999. Some critics think that the giving away of free food at these pantries is leading the donors away from a sense that basic reform measures are required. Janet Poppendieck, *Sweet Charity: Emergency Food and the End of Entitlement* (New York: Viking Press, 1998).

32. Katherine L. Bradbury, "The Growing Inequality of Family Incomes: Changing Families and Changing Wages," *New England Economic Review* (July–August 1996): 55–82; "The Changing U.S. Family," *New York Times*, Nov. 26, 1999.

33. Jeanne Schinto, *Huddle Fever* (New York: Knopf, 1995).

34. Sam Bass Warner, Jr., *The Province of Reason* (Cambridge: Harvard University Press, 1984), chaps. 7, 8.

35. Jessica Andors, "City and Island: Dominicans in Lawrence" (master's thesis, MIT, Department of Urban Studies and Planning, May 1999), 24.

36. Andors, "City and Island," 38.

37. Interview, William E. Luster, director, Office of Planning and Development, Lawrence, Nov. 10, 1999.

38. "The Region's Shortchanged Poor," *Boston Globe*, Nov. 7, 1999.

39. *Boston Globe*, May 19, 1997.

40. *New York Times*, Nov. 19, 1999.

41. *Lawrence Eagle-Tribune*, Nov. 8, 1999.

42. Interview, William E. Luster, director, Office of Planning and Development, Lawrence, Nov. 10, 1999.

43. Interview, Juan Gabriel and José Garcia, May 14, 1999; Andors, "City and Island," 61–66.

44. Interview, Bill Traynor, Oct. 26, 1999.

45. *Boston Globe*, October 18, 1998; Metro West Growth Management Committee of the Metropolitan Area Planning Council.

46. *Middlesex News*, hundredth anniversary edition, Sept. 7, 1997, sec. 1, 10; sec. 5, 9; Laurie Evans-Daly and David C. Gordon, *Images of America: Framingham* (Framingham: Historical Society, 1997), 69.

47. Tracy Kidder, *The Soul of a New Machine* (Boston: Little, Brown, 1981).

48. Falbel, *Demographics of Commuting*, fig. 13.

49. George K. Lewis, *Growing Up in Wayland* (Lincoln, Mass.: Heritage House, 1997); *Middlesex News*, Sept. 7, 1997, sec. 5, 8; sec. 7, 7–8.

50. Sidney N. Shurcliff, "Shoppers' World," *Landscape Architecture* 42 (July 1952): 145–52.

51. Josiah H. Temple, *History of Framingham Massachusetts . . . 1640–1885* (Framingham: The Town, 1887: reprint, Framingham Historical Society, 1988), 48.

52. Interview, Lewis Colten, Sept. 29, 1997; *Boston Globe*, Oct. 19, 1997.

53. On immigration, *Middlesex News*, diversity edition, Apr. 1995; on the African American community, *Middlesex News*, hundredth anniversary edition, Sept. 7, 1997, sec. 6, 8; also Elizabeth Burton, author of the reminiscence *Oh, No, Steven*; *Boston Globe*, Sept. 22, 1996.

54. Joel Millman, *The Other Americans* (New York: Viking Press, 1997), chap. 7. Millman is a child of the Jewish migration to Framingham. An INS raid, "Residents Held in Sweep," *Boston Globe*, *West*, Sept. 23, 1997; a successful Brazilian businessman, interview, Caio L. Galliac, Oct. 2, 1997.

55. *Boston Globe*, June 6, 1997; interview, Lewis Colten, Sept. 29, 1997.

56. Interview, Sarkis Sarkisian, community development director, Town of Natick, Nov. 15, 1999.

57. Interview, Lynda Simkins, farm director, Oct. 7, 1997; Martin Gorsky, *The Natick Community Farm* (Natick: The Farm, 1992); Sam Bass Warner, Jr., *To Dwell Is to Garden* (Boston: Northeastern University Press, 1987), 26–29.

58. Interview, Michael Moran, Oct. 24, 1997.

59. Interview, Steven Smith, executive director, Southeastern Regional Planning and Economic Development District, June 5, 1998.

60. *Boston Globe*, Dec. 28, 1997, Nov. 11, 1998; Cape Cod Commission, *Executive Summary, Massachusetts Military Reservation Master Plan Final Report* (Barnstable: The Commission, September 8, 1998).

61. Interview, Steven Smith, June 5, 1998.

62. *Boston Globe, South*, Apr. 5, 1998.

63. Census Bureau, *1990 Census, Massachusetts*, sec. 1, tables 1, 3.

64. Mertie E. Romaine, *History of the Town of Middleboro, Massachusetts*, vol. 2 (New Bedford: Reynolds-DeWalt Printing, 1969), 61–85, 362–78.

65. *Boston Globe*, Apr. 19, 1998.

66. Interview, Jack Healey, Middleboro town manager, Nov. 22, 1999.

67. *Southeastern Massachusetts, Vision 2020, An Agenda for the Future* (n.p., 1999), 8–9.

68. Cape Cod Commission, *A Decade of Regional Planning* (Barnstable: The Commission, 2000).

69. Interview, Linda Leddy, director, Manomet Center for Conservation Sciences, Dec. 9, 1999.

70. Interview, Donald Connors, Nov. 1, 1999.

71. Haar and Gordon, "Riparian Water Rights vs. a Prior Appropriation System."

72. "Six Moon Hill," *Architectural Forum* (June 1950): 112–15; Five Fields, "Architects Turn Merchant Builders . . ." *House and Home* 2 (August 1952): 88–93; "Snake Hill, Belmont, Mass.," *Pencil Points* 27 (October 1946): 52–66; Conantum, "Progress Report: The Work of Carl Koch and Associates," *Progressive Architecture* 39 (December 1958): 104–18.

FURTHER READING

Eisenmenger, Robert W. *The Dynamics of Growth in the New England Economy*.
Middletown, Conn.: Wesleyan University Press, 1967.

Hitchcock, H. Wiley. *Music in the United States: A Historical Introduction*. 3d ed.
Englewood Cliffs, N.J.: Prentice-Hall, 1988.

Jorgensen, Neil. *Southern New England*. San Francisco: Sierra Club Books, 1978.

Kennedy, Lawrence W. *Planning the City upon a Hill*. Amherst: University of Massachusetts Press, 1992.

Krieger, Alex, and David Cobb, eds. *Mapping Boston*. Cambridge: MIT Press, 1999.

McAdow, Ron. *The Charles River: Exploring Nature and History on Foot and by Canoe*.
Marlborough, Mass.: Bliss Publishing, 1992.

Meier, Deborah. *The Power of Their Ideas*. Boston: Beacon Press, 1995.

O'Connell, Shaun. *Imagining Boston: A Literary Landscape*. Boston: Beacon Press,
1990.

Stowe, Harriet Beecher. *Oldtown Folks*. 1869; reprint, New Brunswick, N.J.: Rutgers
University Press, 1987.

Warner, Sam Bass, Jr., *The Province of Reason*. Cambridge, Mass.: Harvard University
Press, 1984.

Wilkie, Richard W., and Jack Tager. *Historical Atlas of Massachusetts*. Amherst:
University of Massachusetts Press, 1991.

Wilson, Susan. *The Literary Trail of Greater Boston*. Boston: Houghton Mifflin, 2000.

Zaitzevsky, Cynthia. *Frederick Law Olmsted and the Boston Park System*. Cambridge:
Harvard University Press, 1982.

INDEX

Wentworth Institute, 141

Westin Hotel, 141

Weston, 183, 191, 213 n.5

West Roxbury, 163

Wetlands, 194–95

Weymouth, 81

Whaling, 22

Wheeler, Scott, 149–51

White, Kevin, 158

Whiting, Arthur, 117

Whitman, 26, 27

Wildlands Trust of Southeastern Massachusetts, 200

Wildlife corridors, 166, 170

Williams, Thomas, 146

Wilmington, 38, 172

Winthrop, John, 9

Wolff, Christian, 150

Wolfinsohn, Wolfe, 119

Women, 79–80, 114, 117, 208–9

Wood, William, 176

Woods, Roger, 78

Worcester, 4, 166, 184

Worcester Turnpike, 158

Wyman's Garden Center, 187

Xenophobia, xiv–xv, 177

Yankees: bounded towns and, 71; characteristics of, 71, 73; locals, 73–78; politics and, 79, 80–85

Yarmouthport, *191*

Yaro, Robert D., 200

Zayre Corporation, 37–38

Zoning, 209

ACKNOWLEDGMENTS

Any attempt by one person to describe how 4.7 million neighbors live is necessarily an act of imagination. In the instant case, my imagination has been instructed by the many people who offered me the hospitality of an interview. It was these conversations and their suggestions that constituted my regional education and thereby inform the book.

I wish to thank Abe Abadi, John E. Abele, Joseph Ablow, Mary Allor, Alan Altshuler, Jessica Andors, Donato Bartone, Suzanne Belanger, Elizabeth Berg, Chris Biondi, Carolyn Britt, Paul Broadnax, George Cheevers, Jean Christensen, Jack Coffey III, Lewis Colten, John Conaty, Alfred Connell, Karen Connell, Donald L. Connors, Charles Daley, Robin Deadrick, Lindy Elkins, Robert Freeman, Juan Gabriel, Caio L. Galliac, José Garcia, Gail Gardner, Michael J. A. Gavrish, Laurie Geltman, Ruth M. Geoffroy, Frank J. Gersony, Karin M. Gertsch, Glenn G. Gibbs, Cynthia Gordon, Elizabeth A. Grady, Perry Guyer, Marilyn Halter, Jack Healey, Alfred J. Hicks, David Hoose, Loring Jackson, Tony Jarvis, Tim Keyne, Nicholas Kitchen, Richard Knisely, Lawrence J. Lasser, John Leary, Linda E. Leddy, Ann Marie Lindquist, Susan M. Lloyd, David Luberoff, Robert J. Lurtsema, William E. Luster, Kerry Mackin, Angel Martinez, William McDevitt, Dave McKenna, Deborah Meier, Milo D. Miles, Randi Millman, John R. Moot, Michael Moran, Bill Morrissey, Bill Moyer, Michael Nerbonne, William A. Newman, Lynne Nivica, Edward J. O'Brien, Jr., Michael O'Connell, Brad Paul, Ellis Paul, Eugene Pickett, Helen Pickett, Carol Pimentel, Daniel Pinkham, Dick Pleasants, Herb Pomeroy, Larry

Pryor, Watson Reed, Philip A. Rollins, Victor Rosenbaum, Peter L. Rossi, Nick Russos, Shizue Sano, Sarkis Sarkisian, Lloyd Schwartz, Lynda Simkins, Steve Smith, David Soule, Linda Steigleder, Jay Stein, Daniel Stepner, Laura Stepner, Julie Stevens, Sean T. Sullivan, Alan Symonds, Terry Szold, William E. Thomas, Meg Thompson, Bill Traynor, Joan Vodoklys, Larry Walsh, Susan Weiler, Scott Wheeler, Jay Wickersham, Roger P. Woods, Jr., and James D. Worden.

My journeys back and forth across the Boston city region were much eased by the driving of two friends, Hamid Hundal and my former college roommate, the late John Vorenberg. I am indebted, once again, to the skilled librarians of the Rotch Library at the Massachusetts Institute of Technology. The Boston Public Library and the Massachusetts Transportation Library also proved essential. The handsome and informative series of maps has been made for me by an old friend, Eliza McClennen of Mapworks. Chapter 1 appeared in an earlier and different form in the *Massachusetts Historical Review* 1 (1999) 1–19.

Finally, I wish to thank Prof. Judith Martin of the University of Minnesota for conceiving of this project and leading our skilled team of historians and geographers to the challenge.

ACKNOWLEDGMENTS